Selling Life Assurance and Financial Products

Selling Life Assurance and Financial Products

How to Prospect for Clients, Factfind, Present and Sell

Leon Matthews

Copyright © 1994 Leon Matthews

All rights reserved. No part of this publication (except where expressly stated) may be reproduced, stored in a retrieval system, or transmitted in any form or by any means, electronic, mechanical, photocopying, recording or otherwise without the prior permission of the publishers.

First published in 1994 by
Management Books 2000 Ltd
125a, The Broadway, Didcot, Oxon OX11 8AW

This book is sold subject to the condition that it shall not, by way of trade or otherwise, be lent, re-sold, hired out or otherwise circulated without the publisher's prior consent in any form of binding or cover other than that in which it is published and without a similar condition including this condition being imposed upon the subsequent purchaser.

British Library Cataloguing in Publication Data is available
ISBN 1-85252-189-9

Whilst every effort has been made to ensure the accuracy of the contents of this book, no responsibility can be accepted for any financial loss resulting from action taken (or not taken) in reliance of its contents. The information contained in this book was correct as the author understood it at the time of going to press.

Printed in Great Britain by BPC Wheatons Ltd, Exeter

CONTENTS

Introduction		1
1	The Mental Factor	6
2	Preparation	10
3	Prospecting – Finding the Clients	19
4	The Client Meeting	56
5	Familiarising yourself with the client's circumstances and factfinds	88
6	Pointers to the Sale of Certain Products	97
7	The Skills of Persuasion	139
8	Client Profiles and Differences in Client Temperament	147
9	How to Communicate Effectively	153
10	Tips and Reflections on Our Profession	173
11	Conclusion	177
Appendix – legislation and compliance rules relating to the sale of financial products		179
Bibliography		205
Index		207

Introduction

According to figures supplied for a survey published in the June 1991 issue of the magazine *Money Management*, an average 38 per cent of new sales recruits joining life offices left by the end of year one (the latest LIMRA figure supplied at the time was 42.9 per cent), and 54 per cent by the end of the second year. At the top end of the scale the figure was well over 70 per cent. These are worrying figures.

Yet legislation relating to pensions and other personal investments, as well as the increasing number of new financial products coming on to a competitive market, has created unsurpassed opportunities for the sale of these products.

In a society with complex tax laws and Inland Revenue concessions, practically everybody needs, or can find, a beneficial role for financial products: it may be that one could do with more life assurance, or an adjustment to one's pension situation or saving in a tax efficient manner. These products, however, have to be brought to the attention of the consumer public; in other words, they have to be sold. What is more, they have to be sold and marketed competently and in the client's best interests. Each and every product must match a client's strict needs and requirements. There is no long-term future for anybody embarking on a financial selling career unless they adopt this approach.

When selling financial products is conducted professionally the rewards are high and the satisfaction of having served one's clients well is great. Clients appreciate it and stay loyal when served properly. How else can one obtain repeat business over the course of many years?

Yet despite occupying an essential role both in society as well as in the financial services industry itself, the training and professionalism of many financial product salespersons (or financial consultants) has left a lot to be desired. There are of course organisations that do provide excellent financial and ongoing training, which is an absolutely essential prerequisite, and recently the principal regulatory bodies in the UK have taken measures to tighten up in this respect. LAUTRO has announced that all life offices selling their policies through company representatives must have a LAUTRO accredited Training and Competence Scheme. The scheme sets out LAUTRO's requirements for the training and assessment of company representatives by LAUTRO members.

Similarly since September 1992 all new individual applicants to FIMBRA wishing to give independent financial advice have been required to pass the renamed 'Paper 1 Regulatory' of the Financial Planning Certificate. Furthermore, following on from their pilot study on continuing professional education, FIMBRA announced their final training and competence requirements, with the rules coming into effect from January 1994. These include members being required to pass the full financial planning certificate.

It is all the more a matter of regret that one comes across highly knowledgeable and intelligent recruits to the financial sales profession, often from other financial backgrounds such as banking and accountancy, who, despite the potential to become very successful, leave soon after entering the profession, not because they lack a grasp of financial planning and product knowledge, but simply because they lack the selling skills necessary to sell their advice in the form of suitable products that meet clients' needs and solve clients' problems.

Commendable and necessary as the above-mentioned measures are, let us not lose sight of the fact that we are in a commission orientated industry. What is needed is a step by step guide to selling financial products. Given, therefore, the assumption of sound financial planning and product knowledge – now increasingly a requirement of the regulatory bodies, and for which courses and books are available (see Bibliography) – I have long felt that there is a need for a manual that sets out comprehensively the skills and methods necessary for the successful and honest selling of specifically financial products as opposed to products in general. There are many excellent publications of the latter type.

Selling financial products demands skills that are often different, sometimes unique, and requires different degrees of emphasis on some of the other skills common to all selling. It

INTRODUCTION

involves a different type of selling challenge. In financial products one is primarily marketing an idea or concept, often complex, that must appeal as well as be understood, as opposed to something a prospect can see and touch. Secondly, the benefits of what a client is buying may not appear for many years. Thirdly, the product can involve a continuous long-term commitment in the form of regular payments on the part of the client. Even when the idea appeals it can still compete with the temptation to use that outlay for lesser, but immediate, benefits, such as buying a new car or computer.

Selling these products, therefore, involves gaining a client's trust and confidence to a high degree and justifying that confidence over the short and long term by matching the correct product to the client's need. It involves skills of exposition as well as persuasion in prevailing upon a client to accept without regret that which honestly serves his best interests. Above all it places a responsibility upon you to impart the correct advice; you are therefore as much a consultant as a salesman with its concomitant obligations. Only by clearly comprehending and abiding by these guidelines can you hope for a successful long-term career as a financial consultant/salesman.

The methods outlined in this book are based upon my twenty years' selling experience and on research as well as observations and discussions with skilled salesmen of the highest integrity and professionalism. It includes lessons from my early mistakes where, for example, a different word, further clarification or reassurance could have made the difference between success and failure. I have accompanied successful professionals to client meetings and I have observed them making appointments. I soon noted, even taking into account differences of personality, that they had in common certain subtle methods of conducting an interview both consciously and unconsciously. Most importantly, during each and every interview there developed a perceptible respect and trust by the prospect towards the consultant. Such interviews ended with genuine gratitude for the quality of advice and services rendered and not with the prospect relieved to be finally rid of a verbose salesman. Often this was the first time the two had met and the particular client actually comprehended the nature of the product bought, despite previous visits by others.

SELLING LIFE ASSURANCE AND FINANCIAL PRODUCTS

Over the years I have noted that where selling skills are efficiently and properly deployed, the ratio of business concluded has shot up. Where, for some reason, I have failed to perform well it has been reflected in loss of business.

The skills involving the honest and professional selling of financial products can be learned and mastered. The methods outlined in this book will teach you those skills and help you avoid the pitfalls and waste of your time. You will be able to sell financial products successfully and continuously with ever-expanding future sales opportunities and with an uninterrupted flow of prospects. You should also be able to apply those skills within the framework of your own temperament, which is a point that many sales courses ignore.

Let me emphasise that this is not a book on financial planning and it does not therefore attempt to impart a detailed knowledge of financial planning or all the numerous financial products. One must acknowledge, however, that the profession of selling financial products involves a dual proficiency in both the appropriate selling skills and the necessary financial knowledge. In many cases it is difficulty in selling and the consequent inability to generate sufficient income that lead to disillusion and the desire to abandon the profession. Acquisition of the necessary financial and product knowledge is straightforward in comparison to mastering the essential selling skills. I have yet to meet a life assurance salesperson who has left the profession because he or she failed to acquire the necessary financial knowledge.

This book aims to teach you to impart effectively the advice arising from the financial planning and product knowledge that you should already have acquired (or as a newcomer to the profession are in the process of acquiring) from reading and course work.

The descriptions and references to financial products and discussions on financial planning are therefore necessarily within the context of imparting the advice or product that you may judge to be in your client's best interest. Our clients know fully well that we are salespeople but they also appreciate that what was sold to them is what they needed, wanted and had to have explained to them. There is, therefore, nothing in this book that I would keep from them. Professional selling of

INTRODUCTION

financial products is an undertaking that is mutually beneficial to salesman and client.

Throughout the text I have used mostly the male pronoun. This is due purely to reasons of linguistic convenience, and is not meant to reflect in any way whatsoever upon female readers, colleagues or clients.

I hope that with this approach very much in mind you will find this book useful.

1
The Mental Factor

The Correct Mental Attitude
The right mental attitude is undoubtedly essential but I do not believe that it is acquired by sitting in a lecture hall and being whipped up into a state of sales blood-lust by a slick trainer's pep talk. I have sat in on a few of these in my time and quite frankly I have felt uneasy, although I do not wish to decry sales lectures. Some are extremely good, especially those conducted by successful and responsible salesmen of long experience. But there is a better way to acquire the right mental attitude; it is obvious that you need it and it must be a permanent state of mind for as long as you choose to do this job. It can be acquired by bearing in mind the following points.

First, you must make up your mind whether you wish to sell financial products on a steady and permanent basis as a full-time career with its accompanying rewards and advantages. These include freedom to plan your own working day and holidays.

Second, having made up your mind on that score you must fully appreciate that this is a skill you can acquire successfully, and once learned you can become even better as your experience develops. What is more, the skills required do not relate only to selling. They range from a technical knowledge of the products and their application, to social as well as selling skills. You have to be both consultant and salesman.

It goes without saying that you must have confidence in your ability but this confidence will increase as time goes on. Your confidence will enable you to succeed and increasing sales success will also increase confidence in your ability. This will inevitably result in an increasingly positive mental attitude and optimism whereby you will, as a rule, anticipate that each encounter with clients will be successful – and I can assure you that most of your meetings will be successful. Optimism and

THE MENTAL FACTOR

positive attitude are transmitted to clients, who usually respond positively themselves.

I would therefore urge you to fix and keep fixed in your mind a clear image of yourself successfully selling financial products. This mental visualisation of what is perfectly achievable is the most powerful motivator to turning that image into reality. Stamping into your imagination the positive idea of 'I can and I am going to' illustrates the principle made famous earlier this century by Emile Coué, that if you believe that you can do a certain thing, provided that it is possible, then you will do it, and with the least possible effort. The mental and emotional obstacles that would otherwise cause you unnecessary difficulty or distress will be absent.

Probably the greatest mental or emotional obstacle to success in selling financial products is the fear of failure – fear of failure due to rejection after approaching a prospective client and fear of failure to sell upon presenting to a prospective client. Let me tell you now categorically and unequivocally that these fears are totally unfounded. They are unfounded for the following reasons.

First, even though you are bound to have your fair share of occasional failures, there is no reason to fear them if you accept them philosophically for what they are: that they represent part of the natural overall picture of success. Success in our profession can only be measured by an overview comprising both successes and failures over a reasonable period of weeks and even months. You win a few, you lose a few – and not just in this game either. You cannot reasonably expect continuous success in long unbroken consecutive streaks. That is luck. If and when you come across it, good for you. The usual overall picture, however, will be a more realistic ratio of successful sales to failures.

Second, if you learn and practise the correct selling methods described in this book you can certainly expect many more successes than failures. Think of the number of times a parliamentary candidate loses an election before eventually winning a seat. Or the number of times professional sports players lose instead of winning. You are not even in that position. You don't actually have an opposition. What you do have are potential allies which you need to seek out and persuade to that effect, by finding out and conveying to them what they need to do in their own best interest and help them to do it.

So what if you occasionally fail to make a sale, provided that you operate correctly? So what if certain prospective clients refuse to see you? What about all those who will? So long as you philosophically accept your fair share of failures for what they represent – an element in the overall balance of success – you will have removed a major and unnecessary obstacle to that success. Your mental attitude will then have no choice but to be positive. As long as you operate according to the methods outlined here, your successes will more than match your failures. A failed sale will cost you nothing other than the cost of your phone call and travel. Your successful sales will, on the other hand, result in lucrative commissions. So don't allow yourself to be held back from practising a satisfying and lucrative career by false notions and unjustified fears.

You need to have, or acquire, the necessary social skills required for meeting potential clients from most sections of the population and being at ease in their presence without allowing yourself to be intimidated in any way. This does not imply that you need to be an extrovert. Some of the most successful men I know in our field are quiet and introverted but have learned to use these qualities to their advantage. Similarly, extroverts, who have the advantage of not being shy, have to learn to curtail their natural ebullience. Either way, you must like people, and you must like meeting them.

If you are ambitious and determined you can be taught how to succeed in the field of selling financial products. You therefore have every reason to be optimistic about being successful in your chosen field. The result, apart from being in a financially rewarding profession, will be that you actually enjoy your encounters with clients and look forward to them as I do. In short, the whole thing should be fun as well as profitable.

Selling financial products involves imparting technical data to prospects in a manner that prospects can easily comprehend and remember, as well as persuading them that the product in question will meet their needs and requirements. Consequently, the more you develop your communications skills the more effective you will become.

THE MENTAL FACTOR

Professional self-esteem is an essential component of the right mental attitude, and one should always bear in mind that the financial consultant today plays a key advisory role in the personal financial planning of members of the community. His role in meeting the financial needs of an individual is on a par with professions such as accountancy or family solicitors. Provided that you have a reasonable amount of self-confidence, a desire and intention to succeed plus a realistic picture of the financial sales profession, then your increasing success and your own positive mental attitude will be mutually reinforcing. You will be optimistic about the likely outcome of your client meeting, expecting a successful conclusion to be the rule rather than the exception. This positive mental attitude is a powerful suggestive force in encouraging a favourable response on the part of the prospect.

2
Preparation

The successful marketing of financial products requires prior preparation in a number of ways.

Training in Background and Product Knowledge
A most essential prerequisite for advising and selling financial products is a thorough knowledge of all the products that you will be selling. It is a key rule of the Financial Services Act that a salesperson can only recommend a product that he is fully competent to sell. You need to know the technical features, the purposes for which a product is designed, its benefits, and the extent to which it can meet the needs and requirements of a prospective client within the relevant context of law and taxation.

You need to be in a position whereby you are able to discuss products with authority and with the degree of detail that a prospective client may require. However, unless required to do so, your explanation of a given product to a prospective client need not be of the same depth and detail as your own knowledge of that product. You must also be knowledgeable enough to point out and discuss possible alternative products and solutions to your prospect's needs, and their relative merits. You are not allowed to sell any product in which you have not been fully trained and with recorded results.

Through study, reading and attending lectures, you need to acquire sufficient background knowledge of finance, investment and taxation, as well as enough background knowledge of economics and relevant up-to-date law and legislation, so that your recommendations are made within a sound financial context.

Your principals or employers will no doubt arrange lectures by product company representatives, for example, eager to explain their companies' products and their benefits for you to sell (if, say, you work for a broker). However, you need to go beyond this. Attend what additional courses you can. The Chartered Insurance Institute, for example, runs tuition courses leading to its Financial Planning Certificate (FPC) as well as one in Advanced Financial Planning. The Life Insurance Association, which welcomes new members also provides, in partnership with the Chartered Insurance Institute, a progressive range of courses and examinations (see Bibliography for addresses and further details).

It is proposed to introduce a national system of competence testing. The recognised organisations plan to have training and competence standards for their members in place by 1 January 1994, following the SIB plans for the implementation of the McDonald report (1990) on Training and Competence in the Financial Services Industry.

The Life Assurance and Unit Trust Regulatory Organisation (LAUTRO) announced rules that insist for the first time that all life offices selling their policies through company representatives must have a LAUTRO-accredited Training and Competence scheme of a standard that it expects members to achieve. This means that life offices will put their representatives through a period of 'formal training'. In its guidance notes LAUTRO states that it is considered unlikely that the period of formal training could be satisfactorily completed in less than two weeks, followed by a period of intense supervision over a minimum period of six weeks. LAUTRO members 'accredited' training and competence schemes will have to provide for:

- Training in knowledge and skills.
- Supervised practical experience and on the job training.
- Assessment of both knowledge and skills.
- Continuation training.
- Supervisory arrangements to ensure ongoing control and checking of competence.
- Training of all staff involved in the training assessment and supervision of company representatives.

FIMBRA has parallel requirements for its members. The concept of continuing professional education to raise standards

SELLING LIFE ASSURANCE AND FINANCIAL PRODUCTS

of business conduct and to increase professionalism is naturally viewed as very important by the independent (IFA) sector. Since 1 September 1992 it had been mandatory for all new individual applicants to FIMBRA to have passed only the newly renamed Paper 1 'Regulatory'.

During the second half of 1992 FIMBRA was involved in a pilot study that involved recommendations for a personal training programme for each registered individual taking part (involving over 2,000 individuals), which included a mixture of training, updating of knowledge, study for qualifications, skills and experience with a minimum of 50 hours a year spent on Continuing Professional Education activities. This study confirmed support for the idea.

FIMBRA introduced its mandatory Continuing Education Programme in autumn 1993. This requires 50 hours training a year, of which the Financial Planning Certificate counts as 30 hours. This is most important both in formally setting adequate professional standards for those providing independent financial advice, as well as meeting the need continually to update knowledge on a regular basis, as illustrated by developments over the past few years. One is continually encountering changes in pensions, investments, taxation and product details. Such continual education will be recognised by advisers and clients as bringing benefits to both.

The FIMBRA Council also decided that FIMBRA members will have to pass the full Financial Planning Certificate within two years from 1 January 1994. This requirement, subject to certain exceptions (see below), is to include all existing registered individuals.

The FIMBRA Council decided that the final decision of who will qualify for exemption from the above requirement and for what reason will be left to the Personal Investment Authority (PIA). No individual application will be considered prior to July 1994 or the effective date of the PIA. The FIMBRA document says that it is anticipated that individuals would apply for exemption on one or more of the following grounds: alternative qualifications that have been obtained, age, experience, limited or specialist activity. They will also have to supply information relating to other relevant factors about themselves, such as details of experience and information about fitness and properness together with confirmation of being in good standing with FIMBRA.

FIMBRA will also accept Financial Planning Certificate equivalent qualifications from newly registered individuals. These include AFPC, MLIA(Dip), MSFA, ALIA(Dip), AIFP, ACII and FCII.

In addition to Paper 1 'Regulatory' of the Financial Planning Certificate, which was until recently the requirement for newly registering members, the FIMBRA Council has agreed that all new applicants for registration will have to pass the remaining two Financial Planning Certificate modules within two years of becoming registered. Until they do so, they will not become fully registered and will be designated the new category of associate. They will be allowed to give advice and make unaccompanied calls, but must be supervised by a fully registered individual. Fully registered individuals, subject to having at least two years' relevant experience, will then be able to transact business while unsupervised.

LAUTRO members will also be required to reach the FPC Module I minimum standard for all sales staff. However, they will be able to take the CII's own Module I or ask LAUTRO or the CII to validate their own schemes to ascertain whether they meet the required minimum standards.

All the above developments are welcome, both for the achievement of recognised standards of competence and for demonstrating the necessary levels of professionalism. They will also help in improving clients' and other professionals' perceptions of financial consultants and salespersons.

You should study carefully all literature relating to a product – not just the brochure meant for clients but also the technical notes that are often available separately. There are also some excellent books on life assurance and financial planning that cover most aspects of the field (see Bibliography). Such books are available in bookshops specialising in business books.

Make sure that you keep abreast of new developments. If you are a tied agent or product company representative, you should acquaint yourself with any well-known competitor's products so that you are in a position to compare knowledgeably.

The two leading monthly publications in the field of financial services aimed at financial advisers are *Money Management* and *Planned Savings*. With the aid of these you will keep up to date. They contain detailed explanations of all financial products, new developments, news of any forthcoming changes in relevant legislation, performance tables of competing products as well as comparisons and comments. Useful weekly publications include *Financial Adviser*, *Money Week* and *Money Marketing*. If you are advising expatriates, the monthly publication *Resident Abroad* is an excellent source of information relating to their financial matters.

A financial products salesperson is an adviser as well as a salesperson. You need to meet the needs of your clients knowledgeably if you want to keep their loyalty. Any gross errors of advice are likely to be pointed out by competitors, or will be picked up by the clients themselves from the financial press. Apart from the breaching of rules relating to best advice and the possible consequences, the result will be loss of confidence and future goodwill, as well as an unacceptably high failure rate.

It is only after you have gained the necessary background knowledge of finance together with that of financial products and their correct application that you should venture forth to sell. And it is the skills relating to the *selling* of your services that this book sets out.

Appearances and First Impression

Your chances of a successful sale are strongly influenced by the impression you make on your prospect. It is a fact that even if you give good advice you can still lose a sale by a prospect not warming to you. As we shall see later, the most enduring impression is the first impression, and the initial stage of that first enduring impression is your appearance. We shall go into this at greater length later.

As a salesman in the financial sector you are in effect constantly on the market stage, and unless you wear the right 'costume' that market may not make the initial mental association between you and your role. You must therefore look the part associated with your profession.

Your appearance must conform to type and you must look professional. As a financial consultant you should dress smartly and conservatively in a dark-coloured, pressed suit of

PREPARATION

good quality material. Avoid cheap-looking artificial fibres. Your shirt must be of a light colour, whether striped or not, with proper colour coordination between your apparel. Your shoes must be well cleaned and your hair and beard must be properly groomed. You must be and look clean and neat. Similarly, if you are a female financial consultant you need to dress in a manner that projects a serious and professional image.

You need, as much as anything, to look successful. Prospects tend to look up to and have confidence in people they associate with success.

Irritating Traits

Although we shall discuss creating a good impression and non-verbal communication in detail later, it is appropriate to point out that you should try to eliminate any irritating aspects of your outward persona that you may be conscious of, or have had pointed out to you by family or friends. I know of one person, for instance, who once got on his client's nerves by continually fiddling with his forelock and trying to bite his otherwise well groomed beard below the lower lip. Also take care of your teeth and deal with any bad breath. I hope you've got the idea: it shouldn't be too difficult to deal with such fairly minor matters which could put a client off.

Observation and Apprenticeship

With sufficient background knowledge and looking the part, you are now ready for what I consider to be an extremely useful and decisive stage of your preparation for selling financial products: this is to arrange for yourself to observe an experienced financial products consultant at work covering his whole range of activity. You can do this by either requesting your manager to pair you with such a consultant or you can approach one yourself from among your more experienced colleagues. You will find that there is a great deal of camaraderie among financial services salesmen, and a ready willingness by experienced salesmen to help their newer colleagues.

SELLING LIFE ASSURANCE AND FINANCIAL PRODUCTS

A word here about the type of person you should observe at work. They should be experienced and consistently productive salesmen with low lapse ratios whose business sticks. Every salesman has good and not so good periods, but over the course of, say, three months the efficient salesman will have a consistency to his work production.

You do not want to learn from a high flyer with erratic production figures, sky high one month and very low the next, or for that matter one with high monthly production figures, a large percentage of which drops off. Such salesmen are flawed and they may set you an initial bad example. There are unfortunately sales managers who often parade such types as examples to fire enthusiasm in others, especially when they have had a good recent run. You can glean a salesman's background by asking around and observing.

I also suggest that you request your manager to introduce you to more than one suitable person. You can then base your own style on those whose style conforms most closely to your own temperament and personality.

You should observe the telephone manner and selling skills of your experienced colleague. Observe while he arranges his appointments over the telephone – accompany him to clients, and be present during his interviews and presentations. I suggest you closely observe at least four or more interviews. Believe me, there is no better way to learn and it beats many sales lectures you may attend.

Pay particular attention to any aspect of the selling presentation you may feel uncertain about. Note how your colleague puts his client at ease, ascertains his needs and requirements, and how his explanation results in the prospect wishing to buy a certain product, thus resulting in a close.

There should be no problem in arranging these sit-ins from the prospect's point of view provided that your colleague politely asks his permission, preferably beforehand, pointing out that he has a trainee consultant under his wing who will simply sit in and listen.

Finally, discuss with your more experienced colleague how he plans his time.

PREPARATION

Planning Your Time and Setting Your Goals
Plan your time efficiently and further motivate yourself by setting realistic performance goals.

Your time should be divided primarily into prospecting (obtaining appointments) and interviews with prospects. Once you have mastered the skills outlined in this book you will have a relatively high ratio of appointments per number of people contacted, and a substantially higher ratio of sales per number of appointments made. Both these ratios will furthermore improve as you become more experienced. Indeed, the majority of occasions when you will not make a sale will tend to be those where you and your prospect jointly agree that there is no justification for selling anything. There will also arise the rare instances where you simply and justifiably cannot make any headway or reach any understanding with the prospect. In such cases, again, there is usually no case for selling anything, because even if you did there is a very high probability of the case dropping off, i.e. not proceeded with.

Keep records of a client's financial planning and relevant family situation. Note whether he is married, has children, how many and what their ages are. Enter what life cover he has and of what type, any health insurance protection, his pensions situation, type of investments and savings and amount of mortgage payments. Enter any other details that you also find relevant. Record the last date of contact, whether by telephone, letter or meeting, a brief comment as to what transpired and a diary note for an agreed date of future contact, say in six months.

Plan your day the previous evening, jotting down your chores in decreasing importance so that all essential work is got out of the way first. This is an especially useful and practical way of organising your work schedule.

Set yourself a monthly production target and try to meet that target if possible before the end of the month. You can then have the satisfaction of trying to exceed the target if you have met it, or making a final attempt to meet it if you haven't. During December, with Christmas approaching, I divide the month into two. I go all out to do a month's business, if possible, during the first two weeks, given that many clients who agree to be seen try to defer a meeting till the New Year. I then make another effort during the remaining days of the second half. Since December can be a difficult month, it is possible to prevail on certain clients to see them in December rather than January if you appeal to their better nature. Point out that as you will be very busy in January you will be most grateful if they can see you in December since you then have more time to spare. Many existing clients, I find, are understanding in this respect and often agree to such requests. However, do make such requests only to those you judge to be amenable, since it may be misinterpreted by some as pushing.

Product Belief

This may be stating the obvious, but let me go on and say to you that if you do not have faith in any product, don't sell it. You must have faith in the reputation of the company whose products you sell, as well as believe that those products are capable of meeting the purposes for which they were designed.

If you intend to be a tied agent or otherwise become attached to one life office or financial institution, then ascertain how their reputation stands within the industry, how good their products are, and only if you are satisfied on both counts join or carry on working for them; if you are not satisfied then you should move to another organisation that meets these criteria. There is a tendency on the part of sales managers of more mediocre organisations to puff up their company's products to their salespeople and I suggest, therefore, that you make enquiries by reading the relevant trade magazines before you join any direct-selling organisation. After all, why make things more difficult for yourself by attempting to sell bad products compared with the satisfaction of selling worthwhile products to your clients. In all fairness, however, it must be said that there are many organisations, many of whom are household names, whose products and reputation are beyond reproach and which you can be proud to be associated with.

If you are an independent financial adviser/broker, or operating as the authorised representative of one, then you can obviously call on a very wide choice of different companies and their products.

3
Prospecting – Finding the Clients

Many people who could otherwise have followed a successful long-term career selling financial products have in the past been put off, and are still put off, by what they consider to be the daunting prospect of how to go about finding prospective clients – which, in effect, mostly means securing appointments. Let me urge you now not to be daunted. It is not nearly as difficult as you probably imagined. If conducted properly, it has a logic to it that reduces the difficulties and stress associated with prospecting.

There is obviously not much point in knowing how to conduct a sales meeting with a prospective client if you are initially unable to secure an appointment for such a meeting. Note that I am referring only to appointments with prospective clients who are prepared to see you: I am not referring to cold calling in person, such as knocking on doors, nor do I refer to the mindless ringing of people without any prior attempt to qualify them. Such prospects are likely to put off people who would otherwise enjoy a very successful career in financial sales. Also, I do not believe they are efficient methods or conducive to a long-term and satisfying career. (I do not, of course, include here the excellent method of ringing referrals or other qualified prospects whom you have obviously not met before.)

I do not have much time either for organisations who take on otherwise suitable sales staff without giving them any kind of back-up, at least in the form of an initial client list from which to work in the manner outlined below, together with a basic salary or advance against commissions to be earned. This is simply using people as sales fodder without responsibility. It is hardly surprising that many honest, intelligent and potentially good salespeople faced with this situation choose to do something else.

If you operate according to the methods described here, you will have an ever expanding supply of prospects, resulting in a continually expanding client bank which will become your principal business asset. A satisfied client will tend to remain loyal to you, for as long as you retain his confidence and he has your continuing good services. A client will also prefer to continue dealing with one reliable consultant whose competence and integrity he trusts. He will also realise that it is more advantageous to him to have one person advising him and keeping an eye on his financial affairs.

You will need continually to expand your client base, especially when you bear in mind that there is bound to be erosion for reasons such as moving to a different part of the country, emigration, etc. The larger your client bank, the greater your opportunities for obtaining the necessary number of appointments.

Let us at this point remind ourselves as to what constitutes a prospect. A prospect is someone who at the time that you contact him or her has need of, has used, is prepared to use or can profitably use your professional services. This therefore excludes people who are outside this definition for a variety of reasons. Among them are those who genuinely do not wish to deal with you and whom you do *not* bother again. There will be plenty who will want to deal with you.

You therefore need to concentrate on finding people who:

- Need the services that you have to offer.
- Are willing to see you and deal with you.
- Whose interest you can excite to the extent that they want to see you or at least agree to be part of a process that may lead to business. The latter can involve returning a completed application form for life assurance after examining the literature and quotations that you have sent.

It follows from this that the first and most crucial task involved in efficient prospecting is the compilation of well thought-out, qualified lists of prospective clients. These are compiled according to various differing qualifications and categories. The more unqualified or easy-to-compile a list is – such as randomly chosen names from a trade telephone directory – the more it is likely to have been worked by others, and the less satisfactory the results in percentage terms. In fact, with certain easily available lists it is not worth the time and effort.

Conversely, the more exclusive and well thought-out your prospect list, the better the results it is likely to yield. A really well prepared list hardly falls short of being a goldmine. With such qualified lists the number of appointments, or at least expressions of positive interest, per number of calls you make will be high enough to make the effort positively worthwhile and thus motivate you further.

Another important principle to bear in mind is that provided you keep on good terms and do not antagonise prospects, you will be able to contact them more than once and at reasonable intervals, whether or not you initiate a transaction the first time.

The Rules Relating to Unsolicited (Cold) Calling

Those who sell, or would like to sell, financial products within the UK are obliged to confine prospecting and communication with potential clients to within the strict rules laid down by the Financial Services Act. This places restrictions on unsolicited or cold calling.

The restrictions relate both to the manner in which, and the subject matter with which, you may approach prospective clients. Also refer to the notes on Investor Protection and Compliance Rules in the Appendix: you should study all the material on this provided by your employer or principal as well as your regulatory organisation.

Briefly, the position relating to cold calling is as follows. You are allowed to make unsolicited calls either face to face or by telephone, but only with a view to selling certain categories of financial products. For your purposes this must fall within the following classes:

- Most life assurance policies (including insurance bonds) and pension plan contracts.
- Collective investments such as unit trusts (including unit trust PEPS).
- Contracts to manage the assets of an occupational pension fund.

SELLING LIFE ASSURANCE AND FINANCIAL PRODUCTS

- Non-Discretionary Type A PEPS.
- Permanent health insurance and other sickness and accident insurance policies (without investment element, to which the Act does not apply).

With long-term insurance contracts the Act in any case applies to policies that include an element of investment and does not apply if the benefits are payable only on death, as in the case of term policies, or in respect of incapacity arising from sickness, injury or infirmity, or where there is no surrender value (again as in the case of temporary life assurances). You can therefore also make unsolicited calls with a view to selling contracts such as permanent health insurance and sickness and accident policies.

The following code of conduct needs to be observed.

- Unsolicited calls must not be made at unsocial hours. This is understood to mean that you should not call before 9 in the morning and after 9 at night, and not at all on Sundays. Exceptions apply where a prospective client has agreed to take calls outside the specified times, or his working schedule justifies making an exception.
- You must, at the outset of your call, give your name and that of the organisation or firm you work for, and repeat it where necessary.
- You must check that it is convenient for the prospect to talk to you and allow him to terminate the call if he so wishes.
- You must state the true purpose of your call: no vague or misleading statements.
- You must be truthful and factual about the product or service that you wish to sell.
- You must provide a telephone number or an address through which the prospect can contact you to cancel or change the appointment.
- If you are contacting a referred lead given to you by, say, an existing client (as discussed later) you are obliged to disclose who referred you with the referrer's permission.

PROSPECTING – FINDING THE CLIENTS

The Rules of Telephone Prospecting
Before we get down to the rules of qualified prospect lists and contacting them, it is important to learn how to use the telephone to maximum effect. Good telephone technique can make a tremendous difference to the response you obtain in terms of interest and percentage of appointments.

Prepare an honest and practical script. Your opening introductory remarks and the substance of your message when you first telephone a prospect are most effectively delivered when you have carefully prepared what you are going to say in advance. A well crafted introductory script will enable you to sound confident and sure of yourself, provided that you avoid sounding as though you are reading or reciting it. It will also enable you to cover all the relevant points without the risk of omission, or groping for words and ideas during the delivery of your message. Your opening should be done concisely and clearly (see also Chapter 9 on effective communication) Your wording of it can definitely affect the response.

Once you have delivered your initial message you can then speak and respond more confidently to the conversational trend as it develops and help yourself to be on top of it.

The Essentials of a Good Script
This should have the following features:

- It should have a proper introduction. This should clearly state your name and your position, the name of the organisation which you represent and which referred you (in the case of a referral) or a reminder of the connection (as when contacting a name from your organisation's client records). By law this is classed as a cold call and you are legally bound by the SIB or SRO rules previously outlined. Apart from being obliged at the outset to give your name and that of the organisation you represent you must repeat it where necessary. You are also obliged to make clear the true purpose of your call.
- Your script should attempt to create interest by offering a potential benefit This could be for a specific financial product or a more general service such as an offer to

conduct a financial health check (factfind) and make any appropriate recommendations.
- Your script should establish whether the prospect is specifically or by implication interested and willing enough to agree to an appointment. This could take the form of asking whether he would 'like to get together and discuss it without obligation', or whether he would 'like to meet sometime and go over some facts and figures together'. Alternatively you can say: 'Is this something that you might be interested in discussing in greater depth?' Another pertinent statement would be: 'It is difficult to discuss over the phone. Can I take half an hour of your time and explain it in person?' Strengthen your case where possible with offers as in the following examples:

– 'If I can show you how to double your cover for less than twice your current premiums, would you be interested?'
– 'If I could show you how to guarantee up to three quarters of you salary or other earnings in the event of being unable to work due to medical reasons, and no matter for how long, if need be up to retirement age, would you be interested?'
– 'If I showed you how you can substantially increase your company's pension benefits and obtain full tax relief, would you be interested?'
– 'If I showed you how to plan effectively for future school fees, now that your children are young and there is time, would you be interested?'

You can gently nudge the prospect to agree to a meeting (or at least to receive quotes). 'I have time on Monday afternoon or Wednesday evening' or 'I shall be in your area on Monday and Wednesday. May I drop by and see you at either of these times?' If the prospect agrees, arrange a time and date and ring off with 'I look forward to seeing you at 5.15'.
- Your script should have a fallback clause. This is in the event of the prospect indicating interest but not being prepared to make an appointment there and then. This

can involve an offer from you to send quotes first and ring back later. It can also involve an agreement to a request for literature before the prospect agrees to see you. This situation can be converted into a two stage prospecting procedure in order to secure the desired meeting. It can also result in an agreement on the part of an interested but currently unable or unqualified prospect to receive another call from you at a later date. He may feel that he would then be better able to speak to you. Such a prospect may be someone who is temporarily out of a job, short of cash at the moment or simply in a state of uncertainty, and would prefer to speak to you at a later date.

If the prospect does not indicate interest and refuses to initiate any kind of process that may lead to business, or does not want future contact, then thank him for giving you his time and ring off. Please forget any preconceived or ill advised notions about not taking 'no' for an answer and pressing on, hoping to persuade such prospects to relent. You are obliged under the Financial Services Act to terminate the call if the prospect so wishes.

Our task when prospecting is to identify a shortlist (hopefully not too short) of qualified prospective clients. We then further qualify them by telephone enquiry for interest in, and the ability to profit from, one or more of the financial services that we have to offer. If they are not interested enough and are unwilling to take this initial contact any further, then simply move on!

Apart from the occasions when you contact prospects already known to you personally, such as friends, acquaintances and members of your personal client bank, there is no point in pretending that prospecting is a particularly social and pleasurable activity. On the other hand, neither does it in any way need to be a stressful experience when properly carried out.

SELLING LIFE ASSURANCE AND FINANCIAL PRODUCTS

Prospects You Know Who Are Not Yet Existing Clients, and Referrals From Them

Draw up a list of friends and acquaintances you would not feel hesitant about ringing. Let them know the profession you are now in, the financial training that you have received and the range of financial services and products that you can offer. Ask them if they would like to get together with you to review their financial planning: 'It is possible that there may be something I can do for you,' is a good approach. Assure them that they are under no obligation if they agree to a meeting. This reassurance, I believe, is suitable and effective with friends and acquaintances, who more often than not will be pleased to see you anyway, provided that they don't believe they will be pressurised. You will very probably get an appointment there and then! My own sales career started by drawing up an initial list of all my friends, schoolmates and acquaintances residing in London and the surrounding counties, and a most profitable list it proved to be. I was unfortunately not given any client list of the organisation that I worked for at the time to get me started. Even if I had been provided with one, drawing up your own list is too good and easy an opportunity to miss, and will complement the other methods described below. Aim for a list of at least a hundred and preferably two hundred plus names from those you know well to those you know less well.

In most cases the response from old friends and acquaintances, especially married ones, is very encouraging. Here is a subject that they are not averse to discussing and, indeed, need to discuss with someone they know well enough to trust who will not resort, in their minds, to the stereotypical behaviour they may associate with a salesman. The reaction in the overwhelming majority of cases will be something like, 'Sure, come round,' as it was in my case.

If they felt no need to see me, I didn't press. I told them I would send them a card and asked them to get in touch when they needed my services in future. Unless they rang me, I told them I would get in touch again in six months and six monthly thereafter. It is worth adding that if it is all right with them you would like to send them the occasional financial bulletin that your organisation may bring out, or copies of press cuttings that you think they may find of interest. This is useful for

PROSPECTING – FINDING THE CLIENTS

keeping your current status as a financial consultant permanently imprinted in their minds. You will find that after a few months, or possibly much sooner, there will start a dribble of enquiry calls – and a most satisfying feeling it is too.

Bulletins and press cuttings should be sent to all personal connections, preferably in hand-addressed envelopes. Most principals and employers of financial consultants will cooperate in this materially and financially, including bringing out their own bulletin. If not, arrange your own. The personal finance pages of the national press are full of articles that are bound to interest a proportion of clients at any given time, You can enclose an accompanying letter beginning, 'Dear John, As you will recall I am now associated with Sun Star Financial Services. From time to time I shall be sending you material relating to personal finance that you may find of interest. If you should have any queries please do give me a call. Sincerely, Alex'.

If, when you first telephone, your prospect says something like 'I don't believe in insurance or pensions', your response should be along the lines of 'It has its uses', which is brief and effective and gets them to reflect upon the subject. You then point out that of course your field covers far more than just life insurance or pensions.

This type of smart alec is, however, in such a small minority, whether or not you know them personally, that if an appointment does not result you politely apologise for disturbing them and ring off. The day may well come, and very often does, when they will ring you, especially if you keep your professional status in their minds in the manner described above. But I repeat, the declining of an appointment by people you already know will be rare provided that you have previously made a good impression on them regarding your character and integrity.

When you do see the prospect, and after you have finished your meeting, whether you have done business or not ask him who amongst his relatives and friends you can ring and offer your services to. A good way to put it is: 'Who do you know that I may contact with a view to offering my services?' If they are hesitant or decline, then don't press the matter. If they come up with any names get them to agree that you can introduce yourself as their broker/independent financial adviser (if that is your function) or mention the fact that you are their financial consultant. In any case you should secure an agreement at least to mention their name when you ring the referral. What is more, don't place a limit on the number of referrals you are given. If the prospect gives you two, ring two. If he gives you ten, ring ten.

Finally, try to qualify these referred leads by obtaining some information about their approximate age, professional and married status and attitudes. This will enable you to approach them with at least some prior thought and preparation. Thank your contact for the names and do not leave it long before you telephone the referred leads. Don't leave it for more than about a week.

Voice and Telephone Technique
At this point you must learn the rules of the correct voice and telephone technique to use when you contact prospects you haven't previously met. This is not terribly important with the initial list of prospects that are known to you. However, in the case of referrals and other prospects, your telephone sound and manner can make a great difference to the percentage of appointments that you secure or business contacts you otherwise initiate. In fact, it can mean the difference between success and failure.

You should sound confident, positive and friendly but not over-familiar. To sound confident or certain you need to know what you are talking about, and deliver your words with the correct inflection, as explained below. To sound positive you also need to convey a quiet enthusiasm, but not sound as if you have found the elixir of good fortune and can't wait to tell the world about it.

Nervousness can affect your voice. Do not, however, be too stuffy and formal.

The prospect's reaction will enable to you strike the right note within a few seconds.

Voice
You must pay attention to the volume, speed, pacing and correct inflection of your voice, as well as the correct emphasis upon certain words and phrases.

PROSPECTING – FINDING THE CLIENTS

Volume. Do not jar the nerves of the prospect at the other end of the telephone by speaking loudly. Speak softly – it carries greater credibility – but speak with absolute clarity of diction.

Speed and Pacing. Don't talk too fast. This can put off the prospect by associating you with his own mental stereotype of a fast-talking salesman. Listen to and talk at the same rate of speech as the prospect. At the same time pace your speech by the correct insertion of gaps between your words and phrases. For example: 'Good evening Mr Jones. / This is Alan Brodie of Sun Star. I am ringing to let you know that your policy with us is due to mature next month. / You are due to receive thirty five / thousand / pounds.'

Correct pacing aids clarity and the comprehension of your message. If you deliver your words with the gaps in the right places, you will strengthen the impact of the message and add to the anticipation of what follows.

Tone, Pitch and Inflection. Your voice carries greater certainty when delivered with the correct inflection; this is the variation in pitch of your voice as you speak. Anxiety and nervousness will affect one's inflection when speaking. However, if you take care to inflect correctly, especially with the aid of a well prepared introductory message when you first telephone a prospect, you will come across as reasonably calm and confident even if you are not.

This is turn will invite a more positive response. For example:

'Good morning Mr Jones. My name is Alan *Brodie* of Simon and *Hunter* Financial Services. We *note* that you have a policy with Sun *Star Life* Insurance that has an option to *convert*. It is *important* that you are *aware* of *all* your *options* relating to your policy. Would you like to have these options *explained* and have your *instructions* taken?'

You will note that by emphasising the *italicised* words in the above message, it comes across confidently as well as sounding pertinent and credible.

Emphasis. By placing the correct emphasis on a select few key words, you also ensure that you successfully convey the importance or urgency of your message and its principal idea. For example:

'I would like to take the opportunity of explaining to you why a Personal Equity Plan should *definitely* be a part of your personal portfolio.'

'Looking at your file I believe that given your responsibilities it is *imperative* to increase your life cover for a modest outlay.'

'When arranging life cover in your case we need to concentrate on the *highest* possible cover for the *cheapest* premium.'

In prospecting, your voice and choice of words are especially important because you do not have the advantage of eye-to-eye contact and cannot convey a smile at the right moment to project your persona. A good idea is to practise speaking introductory remarks into a recorder. Listen carefully and make any necessary adjustments from a potential prospect's standpoint.

Contacting the Referred Lead

A list of referrals is among the most productive leads that you could tackle. It is very important that you contact all referrals within about a week of receiving them, while they are hot and you are still pleased about having got them. You should be contacting these referrals while you are also working through your original master list.

Contacting referrals soon after obtaining them will help you get into the habit of asking for and phoning them. It will also ensure that there is a steady expansion of your all-important client base.

Don't make the mistake of working through your original master list without asking for or contacting referrals, only then to find yourself wondering where to turn next. If you do not ring referrals soon enough, the leads will get cold and the momentum to contact them will have diminished. The prospect or client who gave you the referral may even have forgotten he gave you the name, if the referral checks up.

PROSPECTING – FINDING THE CLIENTS

When you ring the referred lead, introduce yourself by name, state the name of the organisation you work for, your function within it – such as 'authorised representative' – and mention the introducer. Try to create interest. For example: 'My name is John Smith and I am the authorised representative of Company X. I am the financial planning adviser to Mr Michael Johnson. When I met him last week to review his pension (and/or other financial) arrangements he mentioned you as someone who may be interested in using my services. Would you care to make an appointment to review your financial planning? I assure you there would be no obligation on your part.' If you feel that the response may be positive, you can then offer: 'I could see you for an hour on Wednesday at six thirty or some other mutually convenient time.'

An alternative script, after the introduction, could go along the following lines. 'I was with Mr Michael Johnson last Wednesday planning his pension (or some other aspect of financial planning). Would you like to meet me for about half an hour for me to do a factfind, to see if there is anything we can do for you? I do assure you that you are under no obligation. If I do come up with any recommendations I can come back to you with the appropriate quotes.' There should be no vague or possibly misleading statements such as reducing his tax bill.

Having introduced yourself and hopefully secured an agreement to a meeting, you have now undertaken the most important first step on the road to a possibly successful business conclusion. Also, since most other categories of prospects that you will be contacting by phone will know you or your organisation, ringing them will be easier.

As I have already mentioned, the referred lead system described above is a most effective method of prospecting. It is practised by nearly all successful salespersons of life assurance and financial products. It also results in an ever-expanding portfolio of clients, so useful and vital for an uninterrupted flow of future business.

Assuming that the prospect agrees to see you at the appointed time, simply say that you look forward to seeing him and hang up. If he declines to see you, tell him that you would like to send him a card with the occasional item of interest, and suggest that he may care to get in touch if he requires your services. You should also add that you would like to phone him every six months to a year to enquire whether you can be of help.

Your offer to ring periodically should get a positive response in the overwhelming majority of cases. In fact, the prospect will often confirm the time lapse of his choice with a statement like 'A year (or six months) would be fine'.

On the odd occasion the prospect may say that he or she already has a financial adviser thank you very much, and that there would not be much point. Even then, I point out that if in future he cares to compare any recommendations or quotes that his adviser and I can each come up with, he would be serving his own best interests by taking up whichever suggestion suits him best. 'That way you can get both of us to work for our money,' I add good-humouredly. 'Anyway,' I say, 'I'll drop you a card.' This again hardly ever fails to elicit an agreement. I remember many instances when I have received calls and letters from such people with requests for advice or information that has resulted in business.

A not infrequent response is: 'Can you send me literature?' A correct response is to say: 'I was hoping to do a factfind covering a wide range of financial planning topics, which is what clients find most useful, and then leave you with appropriate literature resulting from a discussion and any recommendations I might make. Any literature I send you now would be less than useful, unless it is relevant to your situation, which is what I would like to assess. You are certainly under no obligation, I assure you.'

If he says he would like literature on a specific product then say: 'The best thing to do in the circumstances is for me to get you a quote together with the accompanying literature. I will also have a copy of the quote sent to me. May I then ring you a week after posting them to find out your reaction and discuss any queries that you may have? If you are interested perhaps we can arrange a subsequent meeting?' Here again the response is usually keen and positive and in many cases will result in business.

Here let me point out a cardinal rule of selling financial products: it is a game of numbers with the odds in your favour. A given number of phone calls will result in a given number of

PROSPECTING – FINDING THE CLIENTS

actual appointments and ancillary requests leading to an appointment. That number of appointments will, with properly conducted interviews, result in a majority of successfully concluded sales. You should aim for an average of at least one appointment from three to four such telephone calls and a successfully and honestly concluded sale in four out of five face-to-face interviews.

Company Clients That You Have Not Previously Met
Any financial organisation that you may be working for, such as a life assurance company or a firm of intermediaries, should provide you with a list of existing clients and their details. Unless you use such client details efficiently and productively, the company will understandably be reluctant to let you have any more. But you should have the right to use their client bank and develop further business from existing clients as well as, of course, obtaining referrals from them.

Ring the client and introduce yourself along the following lines: 'Good evening, Mr Jones. My name is John Smith. I am responsible for your file at Hunter and Jackson Financial Services. We haven't contacted you for some time and it is our policy to ring you at least once a year. May I make an appointment to review your financial planning arrangements? I would also be able to bring you up to date on topics relevant to yourself, and make any necessary and constructive suggestions. I promise you, you would be under no obligation.'

There will be numerous opportunities to ring such clients. Examples range from reminders of conversion options on life assurance term policies, to the statements of benefits of pension plans and investment policies. In such cases the client will have been written to first, or you may receive the communication to pass on. These are all pegs to hang your hat on. In the first example above, ring up and ask them if they would like to have their options explained and any instructions taken. In the second, remind them that pension contributions need to be reviewed at reasonable, preferably annual, intervals and incremented if the ultimate pension benefits are to maintain their purchasing power. The same argument applies to savings plans.

SELLING LIFE ASSURANCE AND FINANCIAL PRODUCTS

There will no doubt be occasions when you will encounter problems in contacting such clients. Problems arise when clients move address without informing the organisation with or through which they took out policies. Other times they may inform you or your organisation of their new address but go ex-directory. In such cases you can often succeed in establishing contact by using a letter like the one in Figure 1.

If prospects have moved away you can write to them via their bank, details of which your organisation will hold on record, usually as a result of the original completion of a direct debit mandate. I suggest you write to them along the lines of the draft letter indicated in Figure 2.

In both cases include a questionnaire (like Figure 3) or detachable coupon for the inclusion of personal details such as address and telephone number. With these you should enclose a prepaid envelope to yourself or your organisation marked for your attention.

If when you ring the prospect he declines to agree to an appointment, tell him you will ring him in six months, but before you put the phone down try what I call the 'last throw' technique. At this point say: 'Before I ring off, Mr Jones, there is one question I would like to ask you.' You should then ask him whether he has a certain product which you suspect – either from the details in front of you or because it may be generally undersold or because of your knowledge about his profession – that he may not have taken up and which he may be unaware of, or as yet has not given any thought to. For example: 'Do you by any chance have permanent health insurance?' If he says he does not and asks what it is, you then briefly but clearly point out the main benefits of such a policy. 'It is an income replacement policy whereby if you are unable to work due to sickness or accident, they will pay you, after a deferred period of your choice an income of up to 75 per cent of your salary for as long as it takes.'

It is essential in such cases to give some details of the principal benefits because you have already had an initial declining of an appointment. The intention is to create sufficient interest to revive the possibility of doing business. You can go on to say: 'I would be very happy to discuss it with you.' If he agrees, fine. If not, suggest that you arrange a quotation based on a

PROSPECTING – FINDING THE CLIENTS

Figure 1.

Name and address of your firm/organisation
Statement of membership of regulatory body

Name and address of client

Dear Mr Jones,

As the consultant looking after your file, it is my policy to contact you at least once a year to enquire whether I can be of any help, and to try to resolve any queries that you may wish to raise with me.

We at this office attach great importance to maintaining an up-to-date picture of our clients' position in respect of their financial planning, so as to be better able to give them the relevant help where required.

I have attempted to contact you by telephone but I notice that you are Ex-Directory. I would therefore be grateful if you would complete the attached questionnaire, including a note of your telephone number.

All information, including your telephone number, will remain confidential with me on file and will not be passed on to any other source.

I look forward to hearing from you.

Yours sincerely,

SELLING LIFE ASSURANCE AND FINANCIAL PRODUCTS

Figure 2

Name and address of your firm/organisation
Statement of membership of regulatory body

To:
Client's name
Bank Account No. of client
c/o Name and address of client's bankers.

Dear Mr Jones,

Re: Existing Life Assurance Plan(s)

We are writing to you via your bankers in connection with an existing Life Assurance Plan that was effected through our agency (or society/company).

It appears that we do not have a note of your current address and as a result we have no option but to write to you via your bank.

We do hope the enclosed information will be of some help to you (enclose literature relating to your organisation plus any details of existing plans, such as a statement of benefits meant for the client). In any event, we would be pleased if you would return the enclosed questionnaire to us, indicating your present address, to enable us to update our records. It is clearly unsatisfactory that we do not have a note of your present whereabouts.

A reply-paid envelope is enclosed and I do hope you will take this opportunity of responding to us.

Yours sincerely,

Figure 3

Confidential Questionnaire

Name (CAPITALS PLEASE) ....
Address ....
....

Phones (Home) ....(Business).. ....

I may move house soon. Please advise me on your special offers on:
Mortgages ....Conveyancing ....

I may be interested in transferring my repayment mortgage to an:
Endowment ....or Pension Loan ....

My present mortgage loan may no longer be competitive.
Please advise on a possible:
Remortgage ....on Releasing more Capital...........

Please advise me on:
Unfreezing my preserved pension benefits...
Improving my pension benefits...
Transferring my old benefits into a new scheme ....
Company Pensions ....Personal Pensions........................

I may have a lump sum to invest......
Possible amount £...........................Tax Rate (%)................................
for income ....and/or growth ....

Friendly Societies

If you or your spouse have not already taken advantage of your tax exempt savings contract, please indicate ....
School Fees Planning ....Personal Equity Plans....................
Other Advice (Indicate what)..
....

Please return this form without obligation to us in the prepaid envelope enclosed.

SELLING LIFE ASSURANCE AND FINANCIAL PRODUCTS

figure agreed over the phone. Tell him that you will send him the quote, some literature and ring him back after a week to discuss it.

You will nearly always get the prospect's agreement to this, and again a certain percentage will result in a sale, pushing up your overall sales ratio. The product that you identify could be a permanent health insurance, the issue of a free-standing additional voluntary contribution plan, the humble Friendly Society plan, or a personal equity plan, to name just a few – in short, any product whose special features and benefits may be relevant enough to the prospect to create immediate interest over the phone. Since the prospect is a member of your organisation's client bank and will usually look to it and thereby yourself for advice, he may well say something like, 'There is something I'd like to ask you' and initiate a discussion over the phone. This will enable you to tell him that you would be happy to discuss it in greater depth and clarify matters by meeting him for, say, half an hour. Again, assure him that he is under no obligation. Point out that once you have assessed his situation properly and got a clearer picture, you would be able if necessary to get back to him after the meeting with further information and quotes.

Once you get in front of the prospect you are on the way to a probable sale if, after a factfind, it is justifiable. If there is a need, and you haven't sold him there and then, you can go back a second time to finalise the matter. This would probably be the case if you had to go back with quotes as described above.

With the increasing sophistication of financial products and the rules relating to Best Advice that apply to independent financial advisers (intermediaries) and tied agents, two call sales are now increasingly common. You can also glean certain advance details over the phone about a prospect's needs, such as his existing level of life assurance cover, the kind of contribution he may have in mind and can afford, his date of birth, and therefore be better equipped with quotations when you meet. These are useful aids for you as well as the prospect, helping him to reach a decision.

If you are unable to arrange an appointment under these circumstances, then offer to arrange for literature and quotations to be sent to him. Tell him that you will ring a week after he receives them to answer any queries that he might have. If, upon ringing him back, he claims that he hasn't had time to look at the quotations tell him you will ring him again in a week. If necessary ring him once a week till you get a reaction one way or the other. The ball is after all in his court and you will not be pestering him by ringing without prior notice. He is hardly likely to be annoyed when he is the one who is procrastinating.

An excellent way, incidentally, of drawing attention to any literature that you have sent is to underline in thick bright red pencil or highlight the key passages in the text that feature benefits and any unique selling points. At the same time draw arrows from the left and right margins of the page pointing to the most relevant of these underlined sentences with remarks like 'Can I draw your attention to this!' or 'Very important!' It doesn't matter that this looks a little untidy – so much the better. You won't find many prospects making the excuse that they haven't read literature they received with red arrows and lines all over the place, which they must initially have looked at with some surprise and puzzlement.

Once the prospect has looked at the quotes you should suggest a meeting when you ring back, in order to clarify matters further. This category of company clients has a comparatively high rate of prospect appointments per number of telephone calls.

Finally, when you do get to see your prospect, never forget to ask for referrals. These should be in addition to your opportunity to sell appropriate products to family members or business partners. Where possible you should always see clients in the presence of such people, both for the additional selling opportunities that they present and to encourage decision-making by the prospect. Very often decisions are taken jointly by husband and wife, and the presence of both may be necessary if you are to complete your sale at one meeting and avoid a call-back. For example, I have found wives to be tremendous allies of mine when selling to their husbands. The closeness of the family relationship does, after all, give them a vested interest in what is being discussed.

Existing Clients You Have Previously Met and Concluded Business With

This section deals with clients you have already met and sold to at least once in the past. They may be friends, acquaintances, past referrals, part of your organisation's client bank or the result of working through other prospect lists. They are clients who are hopefully satisfied with the services you have given them in the past.

In terms of goodwill they are, at the very least, as valuable to you as existing clientele are to any solicitor or accountant. If anything they are even more valuable to you because they represent hard-earned trust and confidence. You will, hopefully, already have made a favourable impression and demonstrated your professionalism.

The opportunities for long-term repeat business here are immense. Clients at different times in their lives get married, have children, get salary rises, change jobs, move house, require pensions, often wish to educate their children privately, need advice on savings, investments and life assurance, and require advice about boosting income in retirement.

At various stages in clients' lives these different requirements need to be catered for. They are in need of good, professional help at these times to help them make the right decisions. They will be looking to somebody for that advice in the financially sophisticated environment in which we live. If they trust your competence and integrity they will obviously look to you as the person who has served them well in the past. As this particular portfolio of your existing clients expands, it opens up repeated opportunities for further future business. The relationship of mutual respect that you build with these clients makes working with them very enjoyable. You will enjoy contacting them and having a chat over the phone as well as periodically meeting them. Some will go on to become good friends.

You should keep proper records of these clients combined with a diary note system. You can do this on your computer, or by opening a file or keeping a card index. This will be in addition to the records kept at your organisation's offices.

Upon first meeting your client you should do a proper factfind (see Chapter 4) relating to his or her financial planning, with a proper review and update on all subsequent meetings.

This record should be entered onto his information sheet and consulted prior to your next telephone contact.

At the end of your meeting you should tell the client that you would like to see him at least once a year if he wants a proper eye kept on his financial planning. Tell him also that you will in any case telephone him after, say, nine months, or whatever useful time scale you may agree upon. Some clients request a shorter time scale for next contact even before you mention it, due to pending developments they have in mind. They could, for example, be moving jobs or be about to change their work status, thereby anticipating that they will need guidance on pension planning at the time.

Enter the next contact date in your diary note system and telephone at that time. A good method is to have twelve filing trays marked January to December stacked in four lots of three, with clients' information sheets clipped to a diary note slip containing the month they are due to be contacted, plus any comments. On the slip you might write, 'Diary note, early March. Moving job at the end of March. Indicates he will wish to discuss pension'; 'Anticipates having some extra spendable income to increase savings contributions'; or perhaps 'Wife expecting. May wish to insure her when child is born' or 'May wish to start savings policy for the benefit of newborn child'. You then place the sheet with the diary note slip in the tray for March.

Apart from time-filing with the appropriate notes, it is very useful to colour code the record sheets of clients with different special interests. You stick a little round red, blue or other coloured sticker on the top left hand corner of a client's record sheet and match the colour with the particular interest or concern of that client. Different colours can represent interests in tax privileged investments, good income producing investment opportunities or new or special investment opportunities for capital growth. You can then, at a glance, identify all clients potentially interested in a relevant product no matter when they are next due for a call, and contact them if you come across anything that might interest them.

Do make sure that you telephone the client without fail at the due time. Your approach should be first to remind the client that you were due to contact him: 'I'd like to see you again, Mr Jones, for a review and possible update of your arrangements.'

If you prefer, or if the client's temperament indicates a milder approach, you can say, 'Would it be possible to get together again to review your situation? There may well be one or two things that need looking at again.' If you have in mind any product from which you believe he would benefit, say so: 'There are a couple of issues I'd like to raise with you.' Also, of course, remind him of any relevant topics that he had anticipated discussing about this time, and point out any forthcoming birthdays where relevant.

In the event that a client declines to make an appointment for reasons of his own, don't risk antagonising him by appearing to push for one. At the time of writing many of my clients were bearing the strain of sharply increased mortgage interest rates. In one day of telephoning from my system, three excellent professional clients who would otherwise have been pleased to see me told me that their spendable monthly income had just been reduced by an average of £200 creating a very tight cash flow. This made it impossible, for the present anyway, in their individual respective cases to increase their pension contribution, take out a further savings plan, and take out a free-standing additional voluntary contribution plan. I said that I fully understood their situation and mentioned that I was similarly affected. I suggested that we had another chat in six months to see what the situation held then. They were all completely agreeable to this and, having passed my best wishes to their respective families and said goodbye, I rang off. It is important to retain goodwill and bear in mind that future business is just as important as current business.

You tend, for obvious reasons, to feel at ease with such clients. When you phone, feel free to raise any matter that you may not have raised before: there may have been a change in legislation that favourably enhances the outlook for a particular financial product, or a new product may have come onto the market which you would like to explain. Ask if you can go round and discuss it fully in person. You may also, upon consulting your records, realise that there is a relevant product he does not at present have which for some reason was not mentioned during previous meetings. Request a meeting to explain it. The goodwill is there. You stand an excellent chance of him agreeing to see you; if he doesn't, then be understanding.

PROSPECTING – FINDING THE CLIENTS

In situations where you feel that an appointment has been declined due to lack of interest, you can always try the 'last-throw' technique. This often throws up some extra business, especially if it is about a product that involves only a modest extra outlay on the part of the prospect.

An alternative and often promising approach is to arouse potential interest by offering to illustrate a possible deal that he would probably not want to turn down. For example: 'By the way, if I showed you how to double your life cover for the next fifteen or twenty years for less than a doubling of your current premiums, would you be interested?' Provided that your offer is correct and relevant to the prospect's situation, you will quite often create interest leading to an opportunity to present.

The methods described in this chapter work and they work extremely well. They are all the more effective for the fact that each prospect is contacted via a preceding connection to yourself such as an existing client, a previous prospect or the organisation to which you belong. By these methods your client bank can be steadily expanded until you reach the stage where your prospecting is aimed more at maintaining the size of your client base and preventing any diminution in your overall number of clients.

Further Prospecting
You may want to speed up the expansion of your client bank, or may need to do so, perhaps because your organisation's client records are for some reason not available, as in the case of working for a new organisation or starting up on your own. If you want to increase your prospecting, the efficient way to do so is first to create more qualified lists of prospects or potential clients. All the lists that we have discussed so far are in effect selected shortlists, albeit of the most profitable kind. You build up your new shortlists by qualifying according to one or more less obvious qualifying denominators. Here you will need to be a little imaginative and perhaps apply some lateral thinking.

The more easily available or obvious a list, such as a trade or professional directory, the more likely it is to have been worked by financial product salespersons and the less likely it is to yield satisfactory results, because somebody has got in long before you. This will be true of lawyers, dentists, doctors, architects or pharmacists, who receive calls from financial product salespeople all the time.

Suppose, however, that you take a certain list like one of those mentioned above or any other trade or professional list, and isolate a certain sub-category of members from that list. Alternatively, suppose you take a list and isolate a specific product that you believe makes it especially marketable to all members of that particular trade or profession.

Let us take a couple of examples. We know that permanent health insurance is more expensive for females than males to take out. If you now isolate the female members of a particular trade or profession, contact them and point this out to them, offering to arrange competitive quotes for PHI, you could make a fair proportion sit up and take notice.

Alternatively, you may create more interest in permanent health insurance by concentrating on a specific trade or profession, whose members are more in need of it than most, such as the self-employed. Similarly, you may notice that a certain category of prospect, such as teachers and local government employees, are especially interested in free-standing additional contribution plans to top up their pensions. With such knowledge you approach as many members of these categories as you can.

When it comes to telephoning these prepared shortlists of prospects, the most effective way I know for getting results is to programme a probable positive reply to a question from yourself. After you have complied with the rules relating to cold calling – i.e. introducing yourself, your firm and what you do – you should phrase your question along the following lines: 'Mr Prospect, would you be interested in applying for (or increasing your) cover to protect your income in the event of illness or accident?' Try and focus on a specific, preferably somewhat undersold financial service such as permanent health insurance which the prospect may not yet have taken advantage of, or which is more than likely to need topping up if he has done so, and which will remind him of his need of it. Furthermore, the service bought to his attention should preferably have the additional advantage (again as in the case of PHI or FSAVCs) that the prospect is himself a direct potential beneficiary (in addition

PROSPECTING – FINDING THE CLIENTS

to any family) and stands to lose out if he does not take advantage of the product.

Once you get to see the prospect you should do a factfind, with the prospect's agreement, confirm (or otherwise) in your own mind and that of the prospect the need for and degree of cover or contribution indicated towards the relevant plan, and also raise any other topics that the factfind may bring to light. This approach can of course be usefully employed also with other categories of client.

The prospecting methods described in this chapter will methodically build up your client portfolio to the level where you will have a sufficiently large client base to keep your diary full. From this point on, the emphasis of your prospecting will tend to be directed at maintaining the size of your client portfolio by replacing lost numbers.

You will also periodically need to increase your client bank to counter a reduction in business from those clients whose finances you have helped to plan adequately for the present and possibly the foreseeable future. You will naturally stay in regular touch with them, but further business will have to wait until next justified. New clients, on the other hand, will probably be in need of active financial planning, with the resulting arrangement of the necessary financial products and services.

Marketing by Correspondence

This method is complementary to the others already discussed; it certainly does not replace them. It is best suited for mass marketing exercises such as contacting a large number of people for your own as well as your company's client bank whom you would not otherwise have time to contact by phone individually.

The Rules Relating to Advertising

The methods outlined in this section fall within the rules relating to advertising. If you are operating and aiming at prospective client markets within the UK, any written communication or correspondence, such as letters, literature relating to services or products and circulars, must comply with these rules. In so far as you the salesperson are concerned, presumably working with or for an authorised organisation or firm operating within the UK as a registered individual such as a company representative, there are certain principles that you must follow if you wish to undertake any mailshot or other advertising campaign. If you also happen to be the proprietor or manager of an authorised firm, you need to study the whole range of rules relating to advertisements by authorised firms in much greater depth and detail than outlined here.

- Any advertisement must first be approved by an authorised person. You therefore need to obtain the approval of your company or principal organisation relating to every detail contained in the copy that you want to send out.
- The advertisement must state the name of the regulatory organisation to which the firm that approved the advertisement belongs. It must not, however, imply that the regulatory body endorses the advertisement.
- The firm must keep a record of the content of the advertisement and the person who approved it.
- Any advertisement that may involve a collective investment scheme (such as a unit trust) also needs to be approved by the trustee or custodian of that scheme.
- Any mailshot or other advertisement must observe all the standards set by the Advertising Standards Authority, as well as the particular rules of the SRO of which your firm is a member.

Any advertisement, which is what a mailshot or other promotional literature amounts to, must not contain any untrue, out of date or misleading statement, promise or forecast. It must also not contain any statement of fact that may not remain correct throughout the duration of the advertising (or promotional) campaign. Neither must it contain any statement of opinion that is not honestly held at the time that the advertising or promotional literature is sent.

Past performance can be published within the advertising literature only if it is relevant and not exaggerated and its source

PROSPECTING – FINDING THE CLIENTS

must be quoted. It must also be qualified by the statement that past performance is not necessarily a guide to the future. Also, any tax implications regarding the product promoted and the conditions under which any tax relief is obtainable must be accurately and clearly stated.

Finally, the wording of any promotional (advertising) literature that you send out, inviting prospective clients to respond, must be in a form that is acceptable to the regulatory organisation.

A mailshot should consist of a brief, easily comprehensible letter not longer than a page; otherwise it will probably go straight into the dustbin. This can introduce the benefits of a certain product or raise a certain topic, such as school fee planning, and should be accompanied by a coupon and reply-paid envelope (see Figure 4). Alternatively, it can take the form of a more general letter accompanied by a reply card listing the range of financial services that you offer, with boxes the prospect can tick to indicate the topic or topics he wishes to discuss (see Figure 5). The letter should invite the recipient to reply if he wishes to discuss any topic without any obligation on his part. The reply card section can be below the letter, separated by a perforation or a 'cut here' line.

When undertaking a marketing exercise for a limited range of products relating to a specific service or topic such as pension planning, it is a good idea to accompany the brief letter with an enquiry form to prompt the prospect into reflecting upon his situation and so to complete the enquiry form and return it. He may have had the vague intention of speaking to someone, sometime, about his pension situation or perhaps he was intending to talk to you about additional voluntary contributions to his pension. Suddenly a letter from his consultant drops through his letterbox, bringing the issue to the forefront of his mind (see Figure 6).

You can raise the response ratio and save postage by limiting a mailshot to a specific category of prospect from the client bank, one you believe is perhaps more in the market for a certain type of product. For example, after consulting your client details you may decide to do a mailshot for permanent health insurance to self-employed clients, whose income is less secure than that of employed people. Their income is, after all,

SELLING LIFE ASSURANCE AND FINANCIAL PRODUCTS

Figure 4

Sample Letter

A FIMBRA MEMBER

Your company letterhead

TO ALL PARENTS

SCHOOL FEES

Those of you who are intending to send your sons and daughters to a fee-paying school at the age of 13 must all be aware of the escalating costs of private education. It is therefore prudent to start planning towards meeting these costs as early as possible. I am taking this opportunity to show you one excellent method by which these costs can be kept to a minimum. This is achieved by means of a specially flexible Endowment/Investment Plan.

EXAMPLE: Male aged 36 next birthday with child aged 2 intending to send him or her to a fee-paying school at age 13.

End of year	No. of policies encashed	Monthly contribution	Illustrated surrender values (Fees provided)
1-10	4	£120	£3,980
11	5	£120	£5,480
12	5	£100	£6,080
13	5	£75	£6,800
14	5	£50	£7,660

Overall outlay: £18,840
Guaranteed benefit during first 10 years: £21,600
Guaranteed investment return after 20 years: £25,008

The plan is flexible and segmented into separate policies.

If none of the segments (policies) are encashed, the maturity value could be £75,700 in 20 years.

Figure 4 (contd.)

All the above contributions and illustrated values, including the maturity value after 20 years, are based on an investment return of 10.50 per cent. The initial monthly premium will reduce as policies are encashed and the proceeds used to fund the required fees.

Alternatively, the same parent could plan for fees by making a lump sum payment or a combination of lump sum and monthly payments.

We can also help you plan for fees that are due sooner than those illustrated in the above sample.

For a personal quotation or consultation please complete the section below and return it to me in the prepaid envelope.

....
Your name and title

To: Midas Financial Services Ltd
      Address

Please let me have details of how I can plan for school fees.

A FIMBRA MEMBER

NAME DR/MR/MRS/MS ....
ADDRESS   ....
           ....
           ....
           ....
HOME tel.   ....OFFICE tel.........................
CHILDREN'S AGES ....

PREFERRED METHOD OF PAYMENT:
MONTHLY.....   MONTHLY and LUMP SUM.....   LUMP SUM.....
NUMBER OF YEARS BEFORE FEES BECOME DUE ....

Figure 5

*Statement of membership of
self-regulatory organisation*

Company Letterhead

FINANCIAL PLANNING

We are able to advise you on the whole field of pensions, insurance, savings, investments, etc. Tick the boxes on the reply card to see what we can offer in the areas that concern you.

Our advice is Independent* and professional: it is given without charge and without obligation.   *Omit if tied agent

---

Name (CAPITALS PLEASE) ....
Address ....
....
Telephone (HOME) ....(OFFICE).................................

I would like a free assessment of my existing life assurance and financial planning, without obligation.

I am particularly interested in:

☐ A general review

☐ Family protection

☐ Lump sum investment

☐ Tax Efficient Saving

☐ Retirement Provision

☐ Free-standing additional voluntary contributions

☐ House purchase

☐ School or university fee planning

☐ Income replacement

☐ Transfer of frozen pension

☐ Permanent health insurance

☐ Other - please specify:

liable to cease from the moment they are unable to work, though PHI is also marketable to employees, whose income if they fall ill will also eventually cease after being on varying degrees of pay.

Other possibilities are school fees planning aimed at couples with very young children; look out for new family arrivals here. The sooner that school fees planning starts the more cost-efficient it is.

A further instance of promoting specific products by post could be free-standing additional voluntary contributions towards pensions for employees (see Figure 7). The letter should be clear and simple with a brief statement of the purpose and benefits of the proposed product or service. It should offer to prepare a quotation by inviting the prospect to complete a quotation request form or the relevant section of an enquiry form before being contacted to discuss the situation in greater detail.

After sending out a selected number of envelopes you will find it very rewarding, after allowing an interval of say two weeks to give a chance for replies to come in, to telephone as many as possible of the recipients who have not replied. Introduce yourself and simply ask them whether they received the questionnaire or enquiry form and whether they need any matters clarified. Ask them, whether they wish to make an appointment to discuss the issues raised. A fair percentage will want to discuss matters and agree to an appointment, although they have not got round to completing the reply card or enquiry form. The mailshot has stimulated an initial interest, which is the first step prior to taking any action. Your telephone call can remove the initial apathy.

A mailshot can also, of course, be used to introduce a new product onto the market.

As a marketing and public relations exercise, reply cards and enquiry forms, etc., can be sent prior to a birthday. One can wish one's client a happy birthday, as well as point out that now may be an opportune time to discuss his life assurance requirements and other aspects of his financial planning.

An individual letter is also an alternative way of making initial contact with a referral. In this instance you should follow it up with a telephone call after mentioning in your letter that

SELLING LIFE ASSURANCE AND FINANCIAL PRODUCTS

Figure 6

Sample Letter

Statement of membership of self-regulatory organisation

Your own letterhead

Name and address
of client   Date

Dear (Name of client)

RETIREMENT PLANNING - THE TAX EFFICIENT WAY

As a member of your employer's pension scheme you can look forward to an income in retirement, but may wish to make additional payments to boost that income.

There are a variety of ways in which you can plan for a better retirement, but using a free-standing additional voluntary contribution scheme (FSAVCS) is a highly tax efficient method.

You decide how much you contribute to the FSAVCS and you decide how your contributions are invested. Contributions made to an FSAVCS qualify for income tax relief at your highest personal rate and your contributions grow free of any liability to UK taxes. When you retire, the benefits from the FSAVCS can be tailored to suit your individual requirements.

If you would like to find out more about how contributions to an FSAVCS can make your retirement planning more tax efficient, please complete the enclosed enquiry form. I will then contact you with a ready quotation to discuss your situation in greater detail.

Yours sincerely

Your name and title

PROSPECTING – FINDING THE CLIENTS

Figure 7

Statement of membership of self-regulatory organisation

Company Letterhead

YOUR NO OBLIGATION ENQUIRY FORM

Name:

Address:

Postcode:

Date of Birth: Telephone — Daytime
                                     Home:

Occupation:

Expected Retirement Age:

One or more of the following is relevant to your employment. Simply tick by A, B or C as appropriate, and fill in the personal details where necessary.

Please return your form to:

A ☐ I am employed and not in a Company Pension Scheme. Please send me details of how I can expect larger retirement benefits at no extra cost to me.
My current salary is: £.................p.a.

B ☐ I am employed and in a Company Pension Scheme. I would like someone to telephone me to discuss my current arrangements and the possibility of supplementing them.

C ☐ I would like a personal illustration of what extra benefits I could hope to receive in addition to the State Scheme benefits.
I am self-employed / in non-pensionable employment (delete as necessary).

My current top rate of tax is:......%

Please base the illustration on a nett monthly contribution of:

£20 ☐   £30 ☐   £50 ☐   £100 ☐   Other ☐

Figure 8

Sample Letter

*Statement of membership of
self-regulatory organisation*

Your own letterhead

Name and address
of client   Date

Dear Mr Jones

I recently had the pleasure of advising Mr John Smith in the matter of his Life Assurance and Pension requirements [or substitute Personal Financial Planning]. I have good reason to believe that he is pleased with my services.

You were mentioned as someone who may also wish to take advantage of my services.

With this in mind, may I ring you next week to find out whether you would like to make a mutually convenient appointment without any obligation on your part, to discuss your personal financial requirements or any specific related matter that you may care to raise with me?

I look forward to speaking to you over the telephone.

Yours sincerely

Your name and title

you will ring him (say in a week) to introduce yourself and to enquire whether you can be of service (see Figure 8).

Finally, it must be stressed that mailshots and letter-writing cannot, as a method of obtaining business, replace personal contact by phone. They can only usefully complement it.

4
The Client Meeting

Meeting the Prospective Client
We now come to the actual meeting with your prospective client. This is my own area of special interest and the part of the selling process that I most enjoy.

Bear in mind that the purpose of the sales meeting is twofold: that is, to serve one's clients and to generate income for oneself. It is also a challenging exercise. Like any exercise it can be observed, analysed and constantly improved upon.

If the principles outlined here are adhered to you should successfully conclude the great majority of meetings with a sale to the mutual benefit of both your client and yourself. The small remaining number of cases where you do not successfully sell will mostly be those instances where, after your factfinding exercise, you voluntarily, and in your own honest judgement, decide that there is no justification or need for recommending any course of action. Your prospect's financial planning may be in an up-to-date and commendable state with little, if anything, that you need to suggest at present. In other circumstances the prospect may prove unsuitable for selling anything to due to personal circumstances that you were not aware of when you made the appointment. That leaves a tiny minority of instances where a prospect is simply impervious to attempts to do business. These are so few that you can comfortably discount them. Consider it their problem, not yours.

You should enjoy and look forward to meeting your prospects, whether for the first time or not. What reason is there not to, after all, if in the majority of instances you can expect at least a pleasant encounter with every prospect of profit? To enjoy meeting people you must make an effort to like them. If you don't your body language may well show it.

THE CLIENT MEETING

A Good Initial Impression

A good sales meeting involves a successful interaction between its substantive and social/psychological components. It is a fact that sales can be and are lost for no other reason than that the salesman and prospect have been unable to find a common wavelength, despite good intentions on the part of both. People can misjudge each other's mood, mentality or character, sometimes even leading to a mild antipathy rather than the desired empathy that is conducive to a successful meeting. This can occur for any number of reasons, ranging from creating a bad initial impression to differences of temperament and even culture. However, in most cases this can be avoided and the positive rapport and cheerful atmosphere necessary for such a meeting can be created. It is your, the salesman's, responsibility to take the initiative in promoting this and here we shall discuss how best to do so. In a separate chapter we deal with the use of selling and persuasion psychology which partly overlaps with this theme. This is aimed at creating in your prospect a relaxed and receptive enough state of mind to give you a positive and fair hearing.

It is a prerequisite of any sales meeting that you make a good first impression. According to psychologists, a first impression takes not more than two to four minutes to make and that once made it is difficult to reverse. As Dr David Lewis says in his book *The Secret Language of Success*, research has shown that once we have come to a judgement about whether or not we like the other person during that short space of time, this conclusion is resistant to change. Since during that very brief period there is insufficient time to control the impression that you make with the spoken word, virtually all the information exchanged is by means of what are called 'silent speech' signals. If your presentation is a good one, this will reinforce a positive first impression. If, however, you mismanage those first few minutes of a first meeting, according to Dr Lewis putting things right is going to prove a lot harder. Even if the substance of your presentation is good you will be working under a handicap.

Do expect to like the client yourself before you meet him or her, and convey through your appearance, social skills and self-esteem that you expect to be liked yourself. Take a genuine interest in the client from the moment that you meet. If you are simply at your natural and comfortable best you are unlikely to go wrong anyway. If you yourself are comfortable you tend also to make the other person comfortable.

Your verbal greeting should be sincere, warm and natural. Your handshake should be neither a bone-crusher nor of the limp, wet-fish variety. Either can put people off. This again has been well established. Pay attention for a moment on absorbing the atmosphere, especially before expressing any strong opinion. Make a quick judgement yourself. For example, what is the prospect's mood? Is he up, down and depressed, happy and welcoming or tense, suspicious and defensive? Is he shy, which can be misinterpreted as coldness, or voluble and extrovert? Noting this enables you to reach and adjust to his mood and wavelength. Note things you like about him. His speech will also enable you to tune into his intellectual wavelength. Is he, for example, precise and analytical, requiring similar standards from yourself, or does he think in terms of more general but nevertheless sound principles? I go into this in greater detail in the chapter on different client profiles.

Essentially, therefore, you need to sell yourself before you attempt to sell anything else, and also have a fairly good idea of the type of person you are selling to.

Upon entering your prospective client's home or office you will, no doubt, be invited to sit down. According to Dr David Lewis, if you are meeting a man you should (if you are male) sit either next to him if you are sitting on a sofa or armchair, or at right angles if sitting at a table. Do not sit opposite him. A man sitting opposite a man subconsciously implies confrontation, competition or conflict, whereas side by side or right-angles implies cooperation and a common goal. However, once two males become friendly or get to know each other well enough to establish mutual trust and rapport, this becomes less important.

Conversely, if you are a male meeting a female prospect for the first time, you should sit opposite her, preferably across a small table. This, for her, is more secure by its implied formality, avoidance of familiarity or implied intimacy, and is non-invasive. Once you get to know a female client well enough you can graduate to side-by-side sitting, implying the

THE CLIENT MEETING

establishment of trust and cooperation. The same opposite position is preferable if you are a female consultant seeing a male client. When seeing a couple, such as husband and wife, do not sit between them; it is better to sit opposite them or at the end of a semicircle so you avoid having to turn your head left and right all the time and can concentrate your influence in one direction. If you have no choice as to where and how you position yourself, then make the best of your given situation, but where you do have a choice I suggest you follow these guidelines which are borne out by experience.

Always leave some space between you and the client to avoid stress arising from invasion of personal space. Also, if at all possible, do not sit in a very deep armchair or in one that places you at a lower level than your prospect. In choosing where to sit it is often easy to take the initiative oneself. You can do it by simply saying, 'May I sit here?' When you sit down, if you find a male prospect sitting opposite you at the other end of the table or room, ask him 'Would you mind sitting over here?' as you would like to illustrate certain points with the aid of a diagram, which could well be true. If the television is blaring loudly ask them politely to lower it. They will in most cases actually switch it off if an uninvolved party is not watching. I have always found prospective clients to be willing and cooperative in these matters.

You will in most cases be offered a drink. It is always a good idea to accept gratefully a cup of tea or coffee; this helps towards the establishment of rapport and enables free and easy conversation.

Factfinding
After breaking the ice with some light conversation it is time to lay the introductory foundation to your professional relationship and reassure the client about yourself and the organisation you may represent. Hand him your card and repeat your professional status as the representative of a product company or an independent intermediary. If you are a company representative, point out strengths such as 'Our organisation is one of the oldest and most distinguished in the country. It looks after so many billion pounds of client's money and has an

SELLING LIFE ASSURANCE AND FINANCIAL PRODUCTS

enviable and consistent with-profits (and/or) investment record.' If you are an independent intermediary, point out the obvious benefits of your facility for researching the market and making recommendations from among a range of companies and their products.

You can now request the prospective client to help you obtain an accurate picture of the existing state of his financial planning. Under the Financial Services Act this factfinding exercise is obligatory, as well as being necessary, to find out what the prospect needs and wants (see page 94). Before you do so, however, if practising in the UK, you should under the Financial Services Act hand the prospect a copy of a Buyer's Guide. This states the difference between a tied agent and an independent adviser, and states which category you (and your firm) belong to. It advises the prospect of your (the salesperson's) and the product company's responsibilities. The Guide will have been published by your employers/principals in an approved form, and you must not alter it in any way (see sample Buyer's Guide in the Appendix).

Again, for those in the UK and operating in accordance with the requirements of the Financial Services Act, this is also a good time to hand the prospective client a Terms of Business Letter, before you actually provide any investment service as an intermediary or the appointed representative of one. This will:

- Describe the services provided by you.
- Refer to the rules of the regulatory organisation.
- State that your firm (or organisation) has undertaken not to transact business in which it has a personal interest without disclosing that fact.
- State the manner in which your firm is remunerated.
- State either that your firm is not authorised to handle clients' money or, if so authorised, specify how such clients' money will be handled.
- State the measures taken to ensure the safe keeping of clients' money (or assets), the client's right of inspection of his assets and relevant documents and records, and that the records will be held for seven years (less in some cases).
- State whether or not your firm holds professional indemnity insurance.

THE CLIENT MEETING

It is preferable to have two copies. Ask the client to sign both, as well as a statement further down confirming that he has received the Terms of Business Letter and a copy of the Buyer's Guide. Keep one copy to be placed with your firm's records relating to the meeting (see Sample Terms of Business Letter page in the Appendix).

Now ask the client the relevant questions that will give you the correct outline of his current financial situation. How much life assurance does he have, what savings and investments, and where? Is he saving on a regular monthly basis under any scheme or policy? If so, which ones and how much a month? Does he have a mortgage? For how much, over what period and what is the method of repayment? How much is the mortgage costing him per month? When does he intend to move house? What is the current state, as well as past history, of his pension planning, i.e. what pension schemes has he been in and contributed to in the past and what, if any, scheme is he currently in? Is he responsible for his own personal, private pension or is he in a company scheme? Does he have any immediate or long-term plans?

Equally important, do not forget to find out what his family circumstances are. Is he married, does his wife work, does she have a pension scheme or any life assurance? How many children does he have and how old are they?

The best way to obtain the necessary information and form the most accurate picture is to request the prospective client to help you complete a set questionnaire. I have included a sample on page 94; you may, of course, devise your own. There are some clients, fortunately few, who may show signs of irritability or tenseness at the sight of a questionnaire. You still owe it to them to obtain a reasonable picture of their position, and for such people I suggest that you quickly go through a checklist of questions and jot down the answers. A sample checklist is shown on page 96. Keep your questions brief and relevant. Make it plain that you simply want a clear enough picture in order to know how best to help him. Listen carefully and respectfully to all he has to say; then ask which of the points raised he considers important in order of priority. Ask if there are any other points he considers relevant to his situation about which he feels concerned enough to want to discuss. He may, for example, be anxious about the cost of private education. You need to draw the client out but do not antagonise by the manner of your questioning. You are, in this way, encouraging him towards a recognition and acknowledgment of his needs in the order of his priorities. This acknowledgment of needs helps motivate the desire to buy. The more forthcoming he is, the more he wants to be helped.

Having received the relevant information repeat it back to him in summary as confirmation of what you have understood his situation to be. You must, of course, be prepared to modify the factfinding exercise because a prospective client who is well informed in financial planning matters may know exactly what he wants and give you instructions to that effect without any intention of discussing matters in any great detail. Under the Financial Services Act this would be an 'execution only' case and you need to make this clear when you report on the case. However, more often than not you are likely to be better informed and more up to date than the client and consequently he is likely to take careful note of what you have to say.

Your whole approach should be, and must be seen to be, the consultant and adviser endeavouring to help the prospect solve his or her problem. You can only do this by being an interested and careful listener, one who the client feels obviously comprehends and sympathises with his particular situation or problem. Note carefully any problems and worries as well as any plans that he may have. An empathy is created when the client feels that you have fully grasped his situation or problem and he will therefore assume that you will know if and how you can help him. Consequently he will be better disposed to listen to what you have to say.

Your principal object is to discover your prospect's needs and any concerns or requirements (such as wishing to invest a lump sum) that he may have about any matter relating to his financial planning. You should find out any short or long-term aims he has that he expects you to help him meet by correct planning and recommendations. For example, he may be looking forward to retiring early and building up a lump sum, while keeping his pension as high as possible; at this point make a simple statement of fact, hopefully to the effect that you

THE CLIENT MEETING

can meet his requirements, which will encourage him to concentrate in a positive manner.

If you cannot honestly meet a client's needs, satisfy his requirements or solve his problems, you should say so. There are rare occasions where circumstances are such that there is no way around the matter or, indeed, any steps that need to be taken. He will respect your honesty and you, in turn, will have created goodwill for the benefit of future selling opportunities. Future opportunities there will be, provided you keep in touch. You will also, more than likely, be given at least two referrals if you ask.

The factfind will enable you to identify your prospect's needs. Is it extra life assurance that he needs? Does his pension need topping up, perhaps in the form of a free-standing, additional, voluntary contribution plan? Has he placed all his substantial savings into a low-interest building society account without any attempt at more efficient savings and investment? He may be a self-employed high earner who will be in trouble if his income ceased due to illness or accident, thus indicating a need for permanent health insurance.

Once you have identified a need, the next stage is to link each need to the appropriate solution or product. This you will do by explaining the main features (i.e. what the product is) and demonstrating the resulting benefits of the appropriate product, or specifically what it actually does for the client that meets or satisfies that need.

You should now tell the prospect what, in your judgement, his needs are, or where you see room for improvement in his affairs and the reasons for them. At this point you should invite his agreement since this strengthens your position. Tell him that you will point out to him how those needs can best be met or a certain situation improved, by explaining the appropriate solution (or product) to each agreed problem. In other words, how exactly your services can satisfy his needs.

It is not enough just to identify each need and the product to meet it. You must now turn that need into a positive desire on the part of the prospect to take up your solution in the form of the product you recommend. It is by matching the benefits to the need, clearly comprehended by the prospect, that you create a desire to take up what you offer – something he needs and from which he will clearly gain or benefit. It is here that we sort out the men from the boys: it is this part of the meeting and how well you conduct it that will determine whether you encounter any objections, and how often, as well as how easily you close. This is an important point in the interview because you should by now have primed him to listen with interest to your presentation of the relevant product or products that is about to follow.

The Presentation

It is the correct presentation of the features and benefits of the product that should turn the need into a desire, thus enabling you to close the sale. Each different situation, of course, has its own needs and may require a different product to meet it. I find saying something like 'I shall explain the product designed to meet the particular needs of your situation' concentrates attention to what is about to be said.

Do not present the client with too many choices, thus confronting him with too many decisions, or he will simply opt out of deciding altogether. Limit the choices to one or a very few that represent the most obvious and suitable solution to his problem. This also demonstrates that you have taken the trouble to grasp and assess the situation and are exercising good judgement. If it is necessary to confront him with more than one choice, then help him to decide by guiding him carefully in the correct order of preference. If, before you have even presented, you are asked simply to leave a brochure instead, point out that you will leave a brochure in any case after you have explained the product and before you leave. Tell him that you wish to make clear the nature of the product and its particular relevance to his own situation.

The key to a successful presentation and consequent sale of a financial product lies in a clear, lucid and accurate exposition of its principal features and especially its benefits in meeting the need, or needs, of the prospect. A financial product, and especially some of the more sophisticated ones that have come onto the market in recent years, can appear complex and difficult to comprehend to a layman. Unless he or she clearly understands at least the basic outline of how a product works, what it can do and why, a prospect is unlikely to have the

THE CLIENT MEETING

confidence and certainty to make a decision and you will therefore not be able to close. One of the more gratifying experiences over the years has been to be told by a newly signed-up client, 'Thank you for clarifying at last how these things worked.' It could be any topic that may perplex a client, ranging from how school fee planning works to a description of, and guidance on, the pros and cons of a pension mortgage.

You must therefore explain clearly and accurately the principal features of the relevant product, as well as emphasise and demonstrate its resultant benefits. Do not omit any relevant feature that may result in failure to convey the accurate and correct overall picture. On the other hand, do not go into so much unnecessary detail that the prospect equally fails to see the wood for the trees. Exactly how much detail is required of you may also depend on the expectations of the client. You can usually glean this from his degree of background knowledge of the issues involved, the questions he asks and his temperament (see chapter 8). You must in all cases be clear and lucid. I suggest you practise explaining financial products to yourself until you feel you are concise, fluent and comprehensible to others.

You really must stress the benefits. This is most important because it is where the prospect's direct interest lies. Unless the benefits clearly serve the prospect's needs he will not buy. You cannot expect him to do so unless he is sure as to what a given financial product can, or will, do for him. Since each prospective client's needs can vary, you should emphasise those benefits that clearly serve and relate to those particular needs. The ultimate test, therefore, of a presentation is to convey successfully the benefits of the product in question and how those benefits will meet his needs and/or requirements. These must be clearly spelt out in plain language. For example, a clear statement of benefits in the case of permanent health insurance could be something like, 'In the event of your being unable to work due to illness or injury, then after an initial deferment period of your choice, such as one month, three months, six months or a year, the company undertakes to pay you £350 per week, literally for as long as it is necessary, and if needs be up to retirement.'

Some sales trainers claim you should sell the benefits only and not the features. I don't entirely agree; at least not in the

SELLING LIFE ASSURANCE AND FINANCIAL PRODUCTS

case of financial products. Unless a prospective buyer of financial products is clear in his mind as to how a product is structured and functions, then he will not be convinced of its benefits. What is more, if he does buy he may soon start having doubts as to exactly how those benefits come about and you may have a cancellation on your hands.

For example, a prospect who is expected to plough hundreds of pounds a month for years into a pension plan has to be told that: (1) the underlying fund into which his contributions go is totally untaxed (feature), resulting in the benefit of a comparatively higher growth rate; (2) it is a feature of the plan that he receives tax relief at his top rate, resulting in the benefit of a much greater investment compared to his outlay, thereby resulting in the ultimate benefits of a higher return both in the form of a pension and a greater tax-free cash sum consisting of up to 25 per cent of the fund. What is more, unless he understands the nature of his pension (investment) fund, which is a feature – be it say with profits or unit linked, the manner in which each type works and is expected to grow – how is he expected to appreciate the legitimate expectations regarding the fund's growth and the resulting sizable tax-free cash and pension benefits it gives rise to?

It is the features that are responsible for the attractive benefits. Otherwise a client might just as well put his money into a deposit account or ordinary unit trust and have access to his capital – and that, as we all know, is a different arrangement for a different scenario serving a separate purpose. Do not, therefore, omit to explain the essential features of the product. Another point to bear in mind is that in many instances it is the uniqueness of certain features that provides the principal benefits. Always, therefore, stress any unusual or unique features that are responsible for any special or enhanced benefits.

Let me illustrate an allied point. Let us suppose that your factfinding exercise has elicited the fact that your prospect has a nine-month-old son whom he may wish to educate privately. He has also indicated, in response to your questioning, that he is prepared to consider suggestions on how to plan for the funding of school fees. You have identified a need – namely, that of helping to lighten the heavy burden of paying for a private education. You have even ensured an acknowledgement of the need by his express willingness to let you suggest a solution. Sometimes, however, that acknowledgement of a need (or problem) that you identify can only come about when you nevertheless go ahead and explain the features and the resulting benefits of a product that will meet that need or solve that particular problem. In other words, a need can be turned into a desire if the prospect acknowledges the *benefits* that will solve his problem.

In our above example you should emphasise, at the beginning, the additional benefits of good timing by planning school fees as long as possible before the fees are due. This additional benefit of good early timing in taking up the product applies to many other instances and, where applicable, must always be pointed out. It is to the obvious benefit of the client, as well as yourself, because it strengthens your own case for selling the product *now*.

Your explanation of the appropriate product, in this case for meeting school fees, could well be that of an insurance-linked flexible endowment plan consisting of a series of policies maturing in different years. These are the lines along which I would present it. A feature of this type of plan is that the premiums are split up into, say, five different endowment or investment policies with the resulting benefit that they can be matured or encashed without surrender penalty and thus meet school fees in the years that they fall due. If the proceeds of any segment or policy do not need to be called upon to pay fees in any given year, it can be allowed to carry on until some later date, thus causing it to continue to grow and accumulate for different future requirements. The policyholder may have had a good financial year and thus be able to meet fees from income in that particular year. Furthermore, the plan is also a life assurance policy with the resultant benefit that in the unfortunate event of the policyholder's death the proceeds of the life assurance can be invested (if required, into an educational trust) to meet the child's school fees. Finally, the policy can be made out in trust for the benefit of the child which means that (in terms of benefit) the proceeds of the life assurance do not form a part of the assured's estate, need not wait for probate and can be immediately directed, if necessary, and in whole, towards the school fees.

SELLING LIFE ASSURANCE AND FINANCIAL PRODUCTS

It is important to grasp that you should clearly spell out and emphasise the benefits arising from your explanation of the features. In the above example the benefit is the funding of a private education as and when the fees are required. It is the comprehension of the features and appreciation of the benefits – i.e. what the product will do for him, what purpose it will serve – that will induce the prospect to want to buy. If he does not comprehend the features, he will not appreciate or be convinced of its benefits. I cannot emphasise this enough. This is especially important where the product has certain unique features: for example, a special feature of a personal equity plan or a Friendly Society plan (including, of course, a pension plan) is that the underlying investment is totally untaxed with the resulting benefit of a potentially higher capital growth. As already discussed, in the case of a pension there is the additional special feature of tax relief on contributions which further helps to enhance the benefits compared to outlay.

Use visual aids where this helps. Also familiarise yourself fully with each product and work out how best to present its features and benefits. Ask yourself what purposes a given product serves. The principal benefit, for example, of a simple term policy to a young mother is the peace of mind bestowed by a high level of protective life assurance obtained at exceptionally low cost while the children are growing up. This peace of mind (at such low cost) is the principal benefit. Should anything unfortunate happen to her, the husband's career and income can avoid disruption or curtailment by the hiring of help if he so wishes. Periodic increases in the cover can be built in to keep up with inflation. Can you think of any young parents who would not appreciate these benefits of such a cheap and simple form of life assurance? This example again highlights the fact that a product can be easily sold, if you correctly identify a generally indisputable need. I can hardly remember an occasion when a parent turned down my suggestion to insure a mother of young children.

As a final example of presenting features and benefits, let us take a Personal Equity Plan. Its descriptive features are that it is an investment in mainly UK equities of up to £6,000 in any tax year. Up to £6,000 may also be invested in PEP unit trusts, if preferred on a monthly arrangement. The unique feature that

THE CLIENT MEETING

gives rise to its special benefits is that the investment is totally untaxed on either capital gains or income, unlike most other investments, and there is no time limit on how long the investment must be held. The result is the benefit of potentially greater capital gains than an investment in equities, which would be subject to tax on both capital gains and income.

Special or unique features that result in special benefits can give rise to unique selling points that make a product more attractive to the prospect. A unique selling point that you may successfully emphasise, for example, against that of the competition, can be the investment track record of the product company (subject to pointing out that the past is not a guarantee of future performance). Other unique selling points can, for example, be cheapness and competitiveness of premiums, or the flexibility of a certain type of policy.

During your presentation note whether the prospect is listening and digesting what you are saying. Invite feedback by saying 'Does that make sense?' or 'Please stop me if you want me to go over it again. It is important that I make myself clear.' Encourage and welcome questions. The more questions you are asked, especially pertinent ones, the better. They are buying signals which, if replied to satisfactorily, all lead towards a close. If you do not know the answer to any given question you must be perfectly honest and tell the prospect that you are unable to answer that particular point on the spot. Note it down and promise that you will enquire and get back to him with the correct reply.

Your replies must be honest. If your product has a disadvantage, first acknowledge it and compensate for it by pointing out an advantage that outweighs the disadvantage. There is an example of this in Chapter 6 relating to a mortgage endowment policy. A product does not have to be perfect for the prospect to buy it, but it needs to solve his problem or meet his need. Keep in mind that successful selling is essentially a process of solving a client's problems.

Finally, recap the benefits and key advantages with a statement like 'I'd like to emphasise the main points again'. Prospects appreciate clarity and accuracy in matters relating to financial products. After all, as my own clients have often pointed out to me, it is not exactly a subject that they spend most of their time thinking about. More often than not they are acutely aware of their lack of knowledge in this field. They are therefore relying on their financial consultant for guidance.

Before you close, make a final check to ensure that the prospect is clear about the product and its purpose by asking, 'Is it clear to you, Mr Prospect? Is there anything you would like me to go over again?'

How to Close
A well conducted factfind and presentation creates its own momentum towards a successful close. The close is simply the final and logical sequence of such a process. Assuming that you have (a) identified a need, (b) secured acknowledgement of the need (before or as a result of your factfind and presentation), (c) presented correctly and (d) resolved all queries satisfactorily, you should be ready to conclude the sale. The prospect should by now want the product.

If a prospect is resistant to buying at this late stage it will in most cases be for one of the following reasons:

- You did not conduct a proper and thorough enough factfind and could not therefore identify a genuine need.
- You did not successfully illustrate or secure the prospect's acknowledgement that there is a genuine need.
- You did not present thoroughly and clearly and therefore failed to convince the prospect of the product's benefits, and therefore that it will solve his problem.
- You failed to convince him that the price is worth paying for the benefits or the solving of his problem.

In such cases, as we shall discuss later, you have to draw the prospect out in order to discover the true reasons for the difficulty and thus resolve the issue over which he remains unconvinced.

Assuming for the moment, however, that you have successfully linked in the prospect's mind the product's benefits to his need, the price he has to pay for the product becomes a lesser consideration and you can now raise the matter. At this point you should enquire about or discuss the maximum amount that he can comfortably afford to contribute or invest (do not use the word 'pay'). He may, of course, not have much choice in the matter as when, for instance, he is about to take up a certain type of mortgage endowment policy for a specific amount. It may also be that he needs a certain level of life assurance for which he has to pay the appropriate premium. Otherwise I usually tell prospects that they should part with the maximum amount that they can siphon off from current income without resenting it. This I find strikes the right note and always goes down well. After bandying about some figures we normally settle for a monthly sum. If it involves a lump sum payment you will find that the prospect usually already has a very good idea of how much he wishes to invest. Apart from it being unethical and against the rules, do not push a client beyond his means for the sake of higher commission or you could end up with a lapsed case. Do not turn up your nose at smaller sales where indicated. Two or three small sales can be as lucrative as one large one.

This is now a suitable stage at which to tell the prospect that you feel you have covered all the relevant points and to ask him if he is happy with your explanation and your suggestions – a powerful closing statement and question, suggestive of confidence and belief in your case. As a courtesy you may ask him whether what you have said is clear to him. During closing you are gently nudging the prospect towards a positive decision and a good way to do this is to ask questions that lead the prospect to give his assent. Your justification for doing so is based on the recommendations resulting from your factfind. His nod and body language, in addition to what he says, will indicate whether he has accepted the product and therefore wants it.

You should now conduct the final stage of the close by suggesting that you take down his details and put the application into the pipeline. Follow this up by saying that you will inform him of its progress, thus implying that it is not the end of the matter even if he has decided, since most applications have to be approved. Bear in mind that closing a sale is the natural conclusion of your factfind and presentation; the result should be that the prospect is happy with what he has bought.

If an application for life assurance is involved, ask the prospect to make sure that he speedily makes a convenient

SELLING LIFE ASSURANCE AND FINANCIAL PRODUCTS

appointment with the relevant doctor if he is requested to go for a medical examination. Point out that the insurance company will pay for this but that the application could grind to a halt if he delays, thus subtly hinting that approval and agreement are not on his part alone. Have your application form ready. Assuming that he gives his assent expressly by saying, for example, 'That's fine; we'll go ahead with that', or by implication by promising not to delay going for his medical if asked, you should start filling in the application form yourself with his replies to the questions that you read out loud. If you have completed the form yourself it is imperative that you then hand it to the client and ask him to check it carefully before signing.

You have now closed. You should congratulate the client on a sound decision. Clients always appreciate a brief word of reassurance. What is more, you must mean it: sincerity is very often accurately perceived. You are also, by implication, expressing that you have done your own job well. You should now hand him a brochure of the product with the words, 'Do please read this later to refresh your memory. Please do not hesitate to let me know if you have any queries.'

At this stage (in the UK) you should also ensure that you comply fully with the rules relating to product disclosure under the Financial Services Act. The client is entitled to, and you must be qualified to give, full product disclosure. You can currently do this by also providing the client with a more technical Contract Information leaflet giving printed details of the product, including specimen surrender values. You must provide this at the meeting or it can be sent shortly after by the product's organisation with the cooling off notice.

LAUTRO has published its new Rules (Bulletin No. 53) on Status Disclosure and Product Disclosure. The SIB has also published corresponding rules. There will be a transitional period before the new rules become effective. Look out therefore for new rules coming into effect and ensure that you comply. Your principals/employers are, of course, responsible for keeping you up to date and ensuring your correct compliance (see also Appendix).

It is advisable at this stage to suggest that the client keeps all policies and documents relating to his personal financial affairs secure and accessible for the benefit of future meetings or queries that may arise at a later date.

You can now move on to any other topics on the agenda arising from other needs that you may have identified. Raise the matter and offer to explain and resolve. Alternatively you can, as I have often done, follow a factfind by presenting each product in turn and effectively closing in the form of obtaining agreement to take one or more of the products. You can then fill out the different application forms one after the other.

The more efficiently you conduct your factfind and presentation, and the more satisfactorily you resolve any prospect's queries, the higher will be your percentage of problem-free presentations and closes. However, your meetings and closes will by no means always be as smooth and problem free as you would like. We shall therefore devote the next few sections to dealing with various obstacles that may arise.

Handling Objections
Objections reveal doubts and concerns which, justifiable or not, are legitimate in the prospect's mind and prevent him from being convinced enough to want to purchase. Normally these would not arise if the presentation had been done properly in the first place, with the prospect's needs and concerns anticipated and addressed. They can also often be interpreted as buying signals rather than an outright rejection of the product. They at least reflect active interest or curiosity on the part of the prospect, which indicates that he is receptive to what you are saying.

Where legitimate concerns do arise they can be handled convincingly to the prospect's satisfaction by following the principles outlined below. The client after all wants to be convinced: he is looking to you to remove his doubts.

You should not view objections as points to be shot down in a debating chamber. That kind of approach would only antagonise the prospect, who is the party you not only have to convince, but in whose good books you need to remain. It is nevertheless true that some prospects do have a habit of raising totally irrelevant objections, and when they do these are all the easier to deal with by pointing out the facts and realities of the situation in their correct context and in a way that reassures them.

SELLING LIFE ASSURANCE AND FINANCIAL PRODUCTS

Your factfinding exercise should make you aware of any special needs or weak points, such as weak finances, that your prospect may have. If, for example, your prospect indicates that he is open to buying some more life assurance due to an expanding family and increased responsibilities but, on the other hand, funds are very tight, you recommend a life policy with the highest possible cover for the cheapest possible premium, and not for any longer than the cover is needed. You do not recommend a sophisticated and relatively expensive variable whole life plan, where he would admittedly get his money back eventually. You thus avoid the potential objection that the life cover he needs is too expensive.

On the other hand, you may glean during your discussion that even though he would like life assurance he is reluctant to have money 'go down the drain', as some prospective clients tend to view the idea of taking out a term policy with no return to themselves. In this situation your job is to preempt the objection and recommend a policy, such as a unit-linked, variable, whole-of-life plan, where he stands an excellent chance of getting his money back and more, when he decides to terminate the policy. Furthermore, he can boost the return by reducing the cover when he has less need of it and keeping to the same premium. Other situations may dictate that you describe both alternative types of policy and let the prospect choose. Such sensitivity to a prospect's needs will often preempt an objection of one sort or another, as in the above examples, and thus obviate the need to backtrack and offer something else which, in a subtle way, interrupts the impetus towards the sale and can even in some cases diminish client confidence.

Assuming you are a salesman/consultant of integrity commission considerations should not enter into your calculations of what to suggest in such cases.

When an objection does arise you should be knowledgeable and confident enough to deal with it in a manner that realistically accommodates the concerns of the prospective client. It is very important also to ascertain whether the objection raised is the real one which is often hidden under the guise of an apparent objection. Note the objection he raises and after dealing with it ask him, 'Is there any other matter that you would like clarified?' He may well say that there is and the

THE CLIENT MEETING

second matter he raises will, more often than not, be the real doubt that was preventing him from taking a decision all along.

Sometimes a prospect may not be sure himself, which is the real item of concern until you gently draw it out of him. You may, for example, have explained and recommended a mortgage endowment policy and he either comes up with the excuse that he doesn't believe in an endowment mortgage, or says that the whole mortgage package will be more expensive than a repayment mortgage combined with a decreasing term policy. Now his real concern, after gentle probing, may well turn out to be that the payment resulting from the low-cost mortgage endowment policy may not be sufficient to pay the mortgage (and leave a reasonable surplus). Once this real concern underlying the objection is identified and dealt with, he may well consider the extra expenditure worthwhile for the sake of the extra benefit. How many bank or building society lenders, you could ask him, would lend money for home purchase if they were not happy that the appropriate endowment policies would serve their purpose of eventually paying off a mortgage? Furthermore, even for a low-cost mortgage endowment the returns projected are intended to leave a safety margin by being able to pay off a mortgage and leave a surplus. There is always the choice of taking up a slightly larger policy than strictly necessary as an added safeguard, which I have found clients are often prepared to do.

It is always important to show sympathy with and appreciation of a prospect's stated concerns. Do not antagonise the prospect by patronising with statements like 'I've been in this business a long time; I know what I am talking about'. Neither, as I said earlier, treat it as a topic for an argument to be won. Soften the impact of the objection initially by saying something like 'Yes I can understand that'. Where it is justified, concede his point on the face of it, especially on a point of fact, but go on and outweigh the objection by expanding your own contention and introducing a new and wider dimension to it. 'Yes, it is not the cheapest endowment or savings plan but the company's bonus (or investment) performance over the past twenty years speaks for itself, although I am not saying that past returns will necessarily be achieved in the future. This is, after all, the only important guide one has for assessing future relative performance. You are no doubt aware Mr Prospect of the difference in pay-out even a one per cent average additional compound growth rate can make to the ultimate maturity value.' I often add, 'You judge a racehorse by its past form even though you can't be certain of its future performance. The same applies to financial institutions.'

You need to make sure that you identify the real substance of a stated objection rather than accept its face value. If a prospect claims that he has enough life assurance, does he really mean that his life cover is truly sufficient for his needs or that he thinks he simply cannot afford to pay for any more, or that he is not prepared to undertake the cost of the premiums because he thinks it too expensive? If, for example, he reckons it's too expensive, a quick quote from my rate book for the cheapest and shortest term assurance has often made a prospective client sit up pleasantly surprised. If a product that you sell has any feature to it that may well be picked upon and raised as an objection, it is better to deal with it early on before it becomes an obstacle.

Bearing in mind that most objections indicate that your factfind or presentation was at fault, when an objection does come up, provided that you have in the first instance advocated the correct product, it can in most cases be satisfactorily dealt with by further clarification of features and benefits within their correct context.

Finally, when you deal with an objection you have in effect done the client a service by clarifying a point or providing information, thus aiding him towards reaching a decision. Look out for expressions of comprehension or agreement in his body language that indicate assent and resolution of the objection – such as a nod or two. These indicate progress towards a close.

I Want to Think About It

Most salesmen view this excuse as probably the most frustrating of all statements a prospect can make. They see all chances of making a sale suddenly evaporate before them. This need not be so at all. You can, in fact, dramatically increase your chances of enabling a prospect to make a decision and,

THE CLIENT MEETING

even if that does sometimes prove difficult, you can still stand an excellent chance of making a sale during a return visit.

The situation usually indicates one or more hidden reservations. Do not appear downcast. Instead appear to be sympathetic and clearly indicate that you understand. Follow this up by saying 'It does lead me to presume from experience that there may be one or more points that you are not sure about. If so, can I take the opportunity while I am here to clarify any such points?' You will probably be asked to clarify something because your offer has concentrated his mind, enabling it to focus on what may have been vaguely bothering him. Briefly note down what the problem is and say something to the effect that this is a straightforward issue which you can clarify. You must now resolve that query to his satisfaction, making sure that all relevant features and benefits are clarified and in context. Ask him if he is happy with your explanation. Assuming that he is and he says so, or you observe him nodding assent, carry on and ask him, 'Is there anything else that I can clarify, Mr Prospect?' You are again concentrating his mind. Given the fact that you have already resolved what was one previously doubtful point, his confidence in you has now increased. He should now ask you about, or raise, any other issue that also prevented him from making a decision. Jot it down and ask if there was anything else. If there was, jot that down too. All too often the first query is of relatively minor importance and a subsequent query is the real stumbling block which you must resolve to his satisfaction before he is happy enough to go ahead. After each query that you tackle enquire if he is satisfied and get a proper, hopefully positive, response. If a prospect indicates that he is satisfied in his mind and has no further queries, you should now attempt to close in the normal way, and you will usually succeed. If you are unable to do so you have no choice, of course, but to ring him back.

It is undoubtedly true that far too many instances where such procrastination occurs arise because of insecurity or simple lack of confidence in reaching a decision, for which the salesperson is responsible and can prevent or successfully deal with to the reassurance and satisfaction of the client. If you clarify the issues involved, demonstrate the need(s), the most important features, the resulting benefits that clearly meet those needs and solve the problem, and if you do so with quiet confidence and enthusiasm, with an efficient, confident, decisive close, then you can also inspire similar confidence in the prospect and the motivation to make his or her decision.

The Deferred Decision

There are some prospects who simply will not sign on the dotted line at a first meeting no matter how clear you make everything and no matter how interested or even desirous they are of the product. Sometimes they will ask you to leave literature with them and tell you that they wish to defer their final decision and will let you know. There may be any number of reasons. They may, for example, wish to discuss the matter with their spouse who cannot be present. This does not occur with any great frequency; indeed, it should happen very infrequently if you conduct a presentation properly and with confidence. It certainly does not mean that you will ultimately lose the sale.

If faced with this situation, make sure that you do not appear to push. That will only antagonise the prospect. Nevertheless, do check again that the prospect has fully comprehended the main features and all the benefits of the product. You should also be happy in your mind that he acknowledges the need or problem to be solved. Ask him if there is any matter that he would like you to go over again. If there are any hidden objections, which may well explain the hesitancy, it is better to draw them out now and deal with them even at this late stage.

If the prospect seems happy enough with your presentation and recommended product solution, acknowledge his wish to defer his decision for whatever reason. It may be purely psychological, arising from a natural lack of ability to take decisions easily or due to sheer inflexibility with no rational basis for holding back. Always, however, secure his agreement to contact him back. Do not wait for him to contact you. It is most important that you control the communication pipeline. If you leave it to him he may contact you but, then again, he may well not. That may depend on how urgent the matter is for him. The best approach is to say, 'Take the time you need. May I ring you back on an agreed date and have your decision and, if necessary, further clarify any points that you may wish to raise? I manage to keep control over my activities this way rather than wonder who is due to ring me and when. When do you think I can ring you? Would next Wednesday be all right?' I cannot ever remember a refusal to such a reasonable request.

If you are asked to leave a brochure (with or without an offer to let you know) ask the prospect to read it carefully and suggest that you ring him back in a week to clarify any points that he may wish to raise as a result of reading it. Always tell the prospect that if he decides to go ahead, you prefer to see him to make sure that all is clear and ensure that the appropriate documentation is correctly completed.

Having agreed a time and date for your call, mark it down in your diary there and then for him to see and make sure that you do ring back at the specified time. This helps to convey efficiency and seriousness of intention on your part. At this point this is the best you can do. A fair proportion, about 50 per cent in my experience, will have made a decision. Of these, just over half will agree to go ahead and you will go back a second time and conclude the sale. If they haven't made a decision accept it in good humour and agree on another date for you to ring back a second time. Your chances of ultimately concluding a sale will have diminished at this point, but you still stand a reasonable chance of selling, so do not give up.

A significant percentage of these apparently deferred decisions can, however, be successfully resolved at the first meeting with a little patience and probing, drawing out any nagging, uncrystallised doubts and concerns and dealing with them to the prospect's satisfaction. Treat the situation initially as a hidden objection that, perhaps, an incorrect factfind or presentation did not anticipate and prevent.

There is an allied and more positive situation where the prospect expressly agrees to go ahead and take up a product that you have presented, but holds back from actually signing up, either because he is undecided on a technicality, such as the exact level of contributions to go for, or because he wants to obtain confirmation of his decision from someone else, be it his wife, employer (as in matters relating to pensions) or bank manager. He may say something like, 'I'd like to go ahead but I won't sign anything now'. This is a promising situation and there is a way to handle it that works most of the time. Your approach should be, 'If in principle you are agreeable to going ahead, to save me a second trip, would it be possible for us to do the paperwork now and allow me to take away the completed form and hang on to it. I will not put it into the pipeline and I can ring you say on Monday. If you confirm your assent I shall push the application forward. If not, I will return it to you.' This delay does not affect the cooling-off period allowed under the law. Point out that this period of grace is still available after you have put the application forward. If the reason for the hesitancy is, say, the exact premium yet to be decided, then you should request that you be allowed to complete the application form but leave the relevant space for the amount of contribution blank to be entered by yourself later, after you have rung back to find out the figure decided upon. In my experience, you are most unlikely to be met with a refusal. Do not date the application form either until you receive permission to go ahead. Your chances of successfully concluding a sale this way are much higher with a signed application form under your belt and subject only to an outstanding phone call, than if you were faced with the prospect of returning a second time (as in the case of a deferred general decision).

Prospects can also be gently spurred on towards decisions by mention of any genuine deadlines such as forthcoming premium increases or certain expected changes in Inland Revenue rules and financial legislation affecting financial products, that may adversely affect their interests if they delay. These will be taken seriously enough to make a difference to your immediate sale prospects.

It is also useful to mark the records of all existing clients who you know from past experience are especially conscientious in their financial planning and who would welcome the idea of being personally informed by you of any forthcoming changes such as those mentioned above; you can mailshot others if you wish. You will, during the course of a financial year, find occasion to pass on such information that will result in sales opportunities. Also, do bring up this particular point where appropriate when prospecting. I noticed recently, for example, that a certain well-known company sends me its revised premium rates for permanent health insurance in March. If you mention this to prospective buyers before the new rates are due, you will have an upsurge in that type of business just as you would when you ring clients with the suggestion that they increase their life cover before their next birthday.

'I'd Like to Speak to My Wife (Husband)'
Whenever possible you should attempt to speak to husband and wife together on matters that concern them both. Exceptions where this is not possible are when the prospect makes it clear that he or she alone takes the decisions in these matters or where it obviously does not concern any other individual except the prospect himself or herself as in the matter, for example, of pensions.

When you set up your appointment, if you suspect that there may be another party involved in the decision making process, make a suggestion along the lines of, 'Unless you decide these matters yourself, if you consult with a partner, may I suggest that we all meet and discuss the situation together'. You might add, 'Then you can both question me'.

In cases where a prospect that you see alone wishes to discuss matters with a colleague or superior, ask him if he will be going ahead with your suggestions if the other party agrees. Offer to present to the other party also, perhaps together with the prospect.

'I Can't Afford It'
Faced with this situation, you should appear sympathetic and point out that 'It's more a question of priorities really isn't it and a matter of reallocating existing resources?' Make the point that what they contribute or invest each month should be an amount that they can comfortably afford and won't resent. I tell my prospects that if they would care to give me any such figure I will give them a quote, or tell them what I can do for them within those constraints. A good example would be the amount of life assurance one would be able to provide for a set monthly

premium. It is important not to push or lay yourself open to such an interpretation. This suggestion usually produces a figure around which one can work constructively.

When a prospect acknowledges a need, but you recognise is genuinely concerned about his or her ability to pay for a service, the following approach not only works extremely well, but makes a much needed contribution towards meeting the prospect's needs: 'I appreciate your concern. I also appreciate that you agree you have a strong need for (say) protection, which cannot really wait for a convenient time to be tackled. Let me suggest that we take this in stages. Let us make a start by insuring you for the maximum amount that £X (a modest uncontroversial amount) can buy now to give you peace of mind. I can after all cover you for £Y with that. It's my job to keep in touch with you and keep an eye on your affairs. We can keep the situation under review.' Similarly, with say pension planning, suggest that he makes a start or increase – any start or increase (subject to the minimum contribution permitted) is better than no start or increase!

If, after all this, your prospect is still adamant that he cannot afford it the best course of action is to say that you understand perfectly and that he is the best judge of that. Suggest that you call him again in, say, six months to see whether he wishes to reassess the situation. I cannot ever remember a negative response to this last suggestion. In this way you will have left open the possibility of future business and created goodwill.

'I Already Have a Financial Adviser'

My method of dealing with this is to address the prospect's best interests in the following manner: 'Mr Prospect, may I suggest that you put both of us to work on your behalf by obtaining quotes and making recommendations for you to study. You can then give the business to whoever provides you with the suggestions and product that serve you best.' I do not remember any such occasions when this suggestion was turned down.

This is also a good approach to adopt if the prospect tells you that he is due to speak to another consultant after you. Here you should request a second meeting to discuss the

THE CLIENT MEETING

matter again, after he has seen the other consultant. Ask that he makes no decision at all until after he has seen you both, had a chance to compare, and until you have seen and spoken to him again. Should he decline a second appointment, arrange to ring him back to find out his final decision; this will enable you to clear up any queries arising from a comparison of both sets of quotes.

Provided that your quotes and service stand up favourably to comparison, you should, by adopting this approach, succeed in obtaining the business yourself in at least 50 per cent of such instances.

Encourage Presence of Interested Parties

During your meeting encourage spouses or any other interested party to be present if at all possible and if this was not previously arranged. Do this simply by asking your prospect if he or she would like husband or wife to join you. Where such a party is present, never ignore him or her simply because the main contribution to the discussion is coming from the main prospect. Give equal or sufficient attention to the other party present by inviting questions or asking him or her to confirm your assessment of any relevant matter.

Wives can be your best ally when discussing life assurance and family protection. You are, after all, discussing family finance and some prospects receive that extra bit of encouragement from their partner to enable them to reach a decision. Furthermore, you may well be able to sell something to the other partner too. I remember one occasion when a wealthy businessman client called out to his wife who was present in the next room and asked her how much life assurance she thought he should have. Her reply was, 'Oh, lots!' He ended up insuring himself as well as her, since they had young children. Always point out the wisdom of insuring a wife, especially one with young children. This is as important as insuring the husband. All it takes to be able to sell life assurance or any other financial product in suitable circumstances is simply to raise the relevant issues and discuss them in a realistic manner.

Useful Words and Phrases

When referring to a past sale do not use the word 'sold'. Instead say 'fixed up'; for example, 'When I fixed you up with an endowment policy'.

Do not use the word 'pay'. Instead use 'contribute' as in the case, 'How much do you think you can contribute?' Alternatively, use the word 'invest'.

Instead of saying 'start another', use 'increase your contributions'. When contributions can be increased on an existing plan it is better to use the word 'increment', as in 'Increment your plan'.

Some Interview Techniques and Correct Procedure

Talk to prospective clients as an equal and do not allow yourself to be intimidated by any prospect. Never look down upon, patronise or adopt a domineering attitude towards anyone with whom you are attempting to do business. You should be in control of the interview without it being obvious. Your demeanour should, however, convey the clear message that you are the expert in your field and that you would like to use your expertise for the benefit of the prospect. Put yourself in the position of a tutor or counsellor.

If during your meeting you realise that your prospect is either not paying attention, despite your best efforts to hold it, or is plainly uninterested, don't waste your time. Cut the interview short without appearing rude. Having already given him your card (this should be done at the beginning of your meeting) ask him to get in touch if he would like to discuss his financial planning again in the future.

Make it clear, when the occasion demands it, that you have nothing to fear from having your professional judgement come under objective third-party scrutiny. I have often gone to see clients and found myself confronted by a pile of financial magazines, with their recommendations as to what the prospect should or should not do under given circumstances. Very often your suggestions will, in any case, coincide with those of the publication. Where they do not, however, state your views without hesitation and spell out your reasons. If you do so with confidence the prospect is unlikely to ignore

THE CLIENT MEETING

your advice even if he does not act upon it there and then. It is useful to relate examples from other client meetings that are relevant to the situation at hand, in order to illustrate or drive home a point. (An illustration of this is given in Chapter 7.)

On occasion, where I have noticed hesitancy on the prospect's part in fully agreeing with my suggestion I have said, 'May I suggest that you contact your bank manager or accountant and check it out with him? I would be happy to speak to him myself if you wish. I am assuming he would bear me out because I am certain of what I am saying.' Whether he reaches a decision there and then or after he seeks third-party advice, this approach does work because it is so obviously said in all good faith.

Where you have successfully concluded business, let the client know exactly what your next step will be. This might be forwarding an acceptance letter, the policy or the name, address and telephone number of the doctor who will be conducting his medical examination. Inform him in advance of when and where you intend to send them to someone other than himself: you may need, for example, to send the policy document directly to the building society lender with a copy to him. In other instances a document might well be sent to his solicitors.

With every new item of business, promise to keep the client up to date on developments relating to his case as soon as you have news, as well as passing on documents such as policies as soon as you receive them. It is a good idea to deliver policies personally: this gives you an opportunity to re-emphasise the benefits of the product as well as to confirm that the client is happy with it. It is also a good opportunity to obtain referrals from a satisfied client. All this is reassuring to the client.

Make sure you keep your word at all times, especially regarding any task that you offer to undertake for the client, whether it is to obtain a quote, confirm a technicality or simply to phone him back for whatever reason. Just as important is to let him know of any task that you have not been able to complete successfully for reasons outside your control.

There will be instances where, through no fault of either party, you suspect you will not sell even before you see a prospect. Where you perceive that the prospect is not a time waster but a good future prospect it will pay you in the long run to set aside some of your time to undertake what may at the time seem a fruitless journey for the sake of building up future goodwill.

If a client indicates that he is satisfied with a colleague of yours he has previously seen, praise that colleague – for example, call him 'very able and efficient'. Do not knock a colleague, on the other hand, if a prospect complains about one whom he has had previous dealings with. Unless the person was a fraudster or was sacked – in which case you extend profound sympathy and apologise on behalf of your company – you should at least appear non-committal or puzzled and appear to give him the benefit of the doubt by suspending judgement until you have looked into your client's complaint.

Complaints must always be dealt with, even if you are not directly responsible. For example, something may have gone wrong in the administrative pipeline of the insurance company with which you placed the client and he keeps receiving overdue premium notices while payments via his bank are perfectly up to date. 'Computers, you know!' Sometimes, replies to a query your client made may not have been received. Deal with them and be seen to do so. It will help consolidate your reputation in the client's mind.

Where possible get in touch with a client at the time that you arrange for him to receive his final documents. Take the opportunity to thank him again for giving you his time and assure him of your continuing attention.

The Competition and You

Provided that you have won your client's confidence and he is happy with your past services, it is more than likely that he will turn to you for advice again in the future. He will probably be prepared to buy a product from the range that you have to offer even though your product may not be the very best available or the most competitive in the strictest sense. Where the difference is very minor as, for example, between premiums of competing level-term policies, it is likely to be ignored because the goodwill and confidence you command with him may well take precedence.

THE CLIENT MEETING

If you are a tied agent your responsibility to give Best Advice under the requirements of the Financial Services Act means you must recommend the product of your marketing group that best meets the needs of your client. The emphasis by the SRO and the SIB is now moving respectively towards the principles of good advice and suitability. If, on the other hand, a client can get a much better deal elsewhere or your product group has no suitable product to meet his needs, there arises a different moral situation and I believe it is your duty to point this out. You may lose a sale but you also build up goodwill for future business when your product may be more appropriate. Also, if you are a tied agent you may introduce the client to an independent financial adviser and be remunerated for the introduction. Obviously this situation will not arise if you are an independent adviser or the agent of one with practically the whole product market at your feet. However, if you are selling or intending to sell a single company's products the situation does emphasise the need to ensure that you sell competitive products belonging to a company of good reputation and track record rather than allow yourself to be influenced solely by differences in commission or employment perks. In the long run you will be better off selling sound products, as well as having greater job satisfaction.

One often comes across prospects with policies or other products that are inferior to ones that you would have sold. Often these have been bought through a friend, partly out of loyalty. Why not transfer that loyalty to yourself and give better service into the bargain?

5
Familiarising Yourself with the Client's Circumstances

Know Your Client
The Financial Services Act 1986 requires you to 'know your customer' (see Appendix). This means taking reasonable steps to ascertain the prospective client's personal and financial circumstances and requirements relevant to the financial services that you are authorised to provide. The Act also requires that the financial adviser should have reasonable grounds for assuming that the prospective client can meet the financial liabilities of any transaction that he undertakes at your suggestion, and also that he understands the degree of risk involved.

The best way to 'know your customer' as required by the Act is to carry out a methodical factfinding exercise with the aid of a questionnaire. If you explain to your client why you need to ask all these questions you will find that there is usually no problem in obtaining the required information. The questionnaire can be along the lines suggested on page 94.

If the prospective client is unwilling to submit himself to a detailed factfinding questionnaire then I suggest that you use a briefer approach and obtain details according to the topics set out in the shorter client details list set out on page 96 below. If the client wishes to confine himself to a specific topic relating to his financial affairs, such as only his life assurance or pension requirements, or instructs you to provide a specific service such as setting up a personal pension plan, then you should make this clear in the report that accompanies the completed application form and other relevant papers to your principal or employer.

FAMILIARISING YOURSELF WITH THE CLIENT'S CIRCUMSTANCES

Best Advice
Having ascertained your prospective client's financial and personal position as best you can, then in the light of the knowledge gained and having regard to any relevant information which you ought reasonably to have known, you are consequently required to give 'best advice'. This means that you are required to ascertain what is most appropriate for your prospective client and to give well informed and conscientiously thought-out advice. The information on which you base your advice needs to be up to date. You need to be especially careful to avoid suggesting that percentage returns achieved in the past will necessarily be achieved in the future, but you can justifiably point out that past performance is relevant in assessing future performance.

Do be careful that your specific recommendations are suitable for the prospect, although the rules under the Financial Services Act do recognise that there is not necessarily one best solution to each case. If a client requests a specific product which you believe is less than suitable, make that fact known, also in writing, and proceed only if the client insists. If you are a tied agent or an appointed representative of one, you can only offer a suitable financial product, provided by the business whose agent you are, whereas if you are an independent adviser or an authorised representative of one, you are required to offer those investments which are considered best on the market and which meet the prospective client's requirements.

'Best advice' also means you need to be satisfied that no other life assurance company or unit trust management group would offer better terms, including taking into account such factors as underwriting policy, safety and other characteristics. This involves, for example, being informed about current terms in the market for particular products, such as annuities and term assurance, as well as keeping up to date on other aspects of the market.

Strategy
A vital task when assessing a prospective client's financial situation, before making any changes or additions, is to see if all existing financial arrangements are as they should be, which

they rarely are, both in terms of sufficiency and justifying their existence and in terms of giving good value for money. Below I draw attention to the range of important financial arrangements, investments and types of insurance cover that you should check.

Pensions
Many people are not sure about what sort of purchasing power their pension will have. To work out the total entitlement upon retirement, take into account the state pension, an estimate of the benefits arising from company pension schemes and any personal pension plans. The numerical estimate arrived at – say, £65,000 per annum – might look good on paper but over 20 or 25 years its real value will be significantly reduced by inflation. Furthermore, a client might not even be currently contributing to a pension plan. Where you have calculated correctly that the client's pension benefits will be poor, you should suggest extra contributions either through a personal pension plan or a free-standing AVC scheme (or the company's own scheme). Clients who are not already in a pension scheme should be recommended to take out a personal pension plan.

Contracting out of the State Earnings-Related Pension Scheme is still worthwhile for younger people – say for women under 40 and men under 45 – though here individual circumstances must be taken into account.

Life policies
Careful consideration needs to be given to the level and sufficiency of life assurance cover. Assess carefully the client's family responsibilities and bear in mind that term assurance is both cheap and easily saleable. Most people are in reality underinsured and if this is the case with your client you should point this out. A good criterion is whether a widow (or widower) can live comfortably on the income that the total invested proceeds of the life assurance policies would generate.

You should check as to who exactly are the beneficiaries of a life assurance policy. The life cover provided by company schemes, for example, are paid at the discretion of the trustees. The trustees need to know who the employee wants to benefit from the lump sum of up to four times salary. You would do

FAMILIARISING YOURSELF WITH THE CLIENT'S CIRCUMSTANCES

well to advise self-employed people or employees who take out their own personal pension plans to add on term assurance to their pension plans, and obtain tax relief on the premiums.

Private health insurance
Illness can be devastating to the prospect's, and his family's, financial and personal situation. A prospect and his family need to consider the cost of replacing, as far as possible, the loss of income if the breadwinner is unable to earn due to illness or accident. Careful consideration needs to be given to the deferment period before benefit is paid out, during which the policyholder and his dependents will need to survive without receiving payment. The longer the deferment, obviously the cheaper the premiums for any given benefit cover. Bear in mind also the relatively new disease insurance which pays out a lump sum on diagnosis of a critical illness to help meet costs.

Savings
It is important to establish how a client is currently saving, if at all. Savings from current income should basically be split into three: short-term savings on interest where the money is readily available in an emergency; medium-term savings, say up to five years on deposit at highest possible interest, preferably paid gross as with a TESSA; and long-term savings for a minimum of ten years through investment schemes such as endowments offering the prospect of a better investment return than interest. Here, bear in mind the tax exempt Friendly Society plans which allow an individual to invest up to £18 per month (at time of writing) in a tax-exempt fund. Also note that these plans are once again available for children.

Investments
The splitting of regular savings mentioned above also applies to any lump sum investments you recommend. It is most important to ascertain from a prospective client when he will require the proceeds of an investment or the income from it. If a prospect indicates that he may need the money in a few months or even in a year or two, you should certainly not recommend a unit trust or personal equity plan. Here again, capital that may be required in the short term should be placed

SELLING LIFE ASSURANCE AND FINANCIAL PRODUCTS

in a building society interest-bearing account. Money that will not be required for, say, five years or more can be split between a safe tax-advantageous interest-bearing account such as a TESSA which you can help set up for the client, and unit trusts, PEPs or insurance bonds. The nature of these investments must be made clear, especially that they need to be invested over a reasonable period – say up to five years – for a client to look forward to the prospect of a worthwhile capital growth.

When giving advice you need to pay attention to the suitability, degree of risk and outlook for the particular type of fund that you are recommending the client to invest in. What are the client's requirement and what degree of risk is a client prepared to subject his money to? The degree of risk must, as far as possible, be made clear. Do you, for instance, advise him to put some portion of his money into the Far East and Europe or stick to a safer, managed fund with its balance of investments?

Personal Equity Plans with their tax advantages, unit trusts with their spread of risk (including unit trust PEPS) and life assurance bonds all have their rightful place in financial planning. With-profit bonds are obviously safer than unit-linked bonds. Beware of selling life assurance bonds to people who are unlikely to have any capital gains tax liability because the capital gains tax deducted from the payout is not reclaimable.

You also need to be acquainted with the suitability of other alternative investments to the above if you are to give unbiased independent advice. These include National Savings, such as the index-linked National Savings Bonds that pay additional interest above the retail price index for five years.

Mortgages
Examine whether a client's current mortgage is good value and as efficient as it could be. Is he paying higher interest rates than he needs to? If he is, especially with large loans it may be worthwhile to remortgage at lower interest rates, and where suitable to switch to a more advantageous type of mortgage, perhaps a pension or endowment mortgage. Those with smaller loans may find the cost of solicitors' and surveyors' fees outweigh the cost of reduced mortgage payments.

Any remortgaging to lower interest rates should not be done for short-term advantage. You need to help the client weigh up

FAMILIARISING YOURSELF WITH THE CLIENT'S CIRCUMSTANCES

carefully the various factors such as an attractive fixed rate mortgage during times of high interest, the differences between rates, and whether lower interest rates are likely to remain that way. It is also worth considering the standing and record of the lender in this respect. I would consider it justified, for example, to recommend a switch to a lender charging 11.5 per cent if a client is currently being charged 14 per cent. Allow a prospect time to reflect upon any advice you may give in this respect. It may well be that a client justifiably does not want to undergo the upheaval and expense of switching mortgages.

Wills
You should encourage your clients to make a will because if they die intestate their estate may be passed on automatically other than they would have wished. It could even mean that the matrimonial home does not pass to a spouse. At the time of writing, for example, if someone dies intestate the first £75,000 of the estate goes to the spouse. Any balance is divided between the spouse and the children. If there are no children the spouse receives the first £120,000 and the rest is shared between the next of kin.

Liabilities
It is worth keeping up to date on the lending policy of lenders other than those for home purchase. You can then advise a client on the cheapest way to borrow as well as to pay off various types of loan. Often this can involve some life assurance business. Unauthorised overdrafts, it is worth pointing out, are more expensive than those previously authorised.

Contents insurance
You should be in a position to advise on home contents insurance. A prospective client's home contents insurance should cover everything possible. Underinsurance could result in the payout being scaled down when a claim is made. One way to avoid this is to recommend a policy that pays out, up to a pre-set maximum, depending on the number of rooms.

If your employers also do general insurance, the extra business you bring their way will do your reputation good even if you are not entitled to commission for general insurance.

Moreover, you might well be able to negotiate remuneration for the introduction of this type of business.

These notes are intended for your guidance only within the context of your factfinding exercise, and are not intended as specific investment advice to be imparted. You should ensure that you are well versed and up to date in the principles of financial planning, which are not within the scope of this book (see Bibliography).

CONFIDENTIAL QUESTIONNAIRE THAT COULD BE USED FOR FACTFINDING

Personal details
    Age
    Marital status
    Occupation
    Income   Tax bracket
    Retirement age
    Are you resident in the UK?   YES/NO

Family details
    Age of spouse
    Occupation of spouse
    Income of spouse (if working)
      or investment income
    Retirement age of spouse
    Number of children
    How do you intend to educate children?

Requirements
    Are you interested in increasing net income?   YES/NO
    Are you interested in capital appreciation?   YES/NO
    Are you interested in mitigating potential inheritance tax?   YES/NO
    What is your attitude towards financial risk on a scale of 1 to 10?

Assets
    House (private residence)
    Other properties
    What investments held?

FAMILIARISING YOURSELF WITH THE CLIENT'S CIRCUMSTANCES

Liabilities
    Amount of mortgage on private residence
    Amount of mortgage on any other property
    Other debts such as bank loans and overdrafts
    Do you anticipate any capital expenditure and if so when?

Gifts
    What gifts have you or your spouse made within the last seven years?
    If any, please give details and their values.
    What steps have you taken to mitigate any inheritance tax liability?

Trusts, settlements and inheritances
    Are you or your spouse the current or likely future beneficiaries of any will?   YES/NO
    If YES, please give details.
    Are you or your spouse the beneficiaries of any trust?   YES/NO
    If YES, please give details.

Wills
    Have you or your spouse made wills?   YES/NO
    If YES what are its main provisions?

Income
    What is your earned income?
    What is your spouse's income?
    What business profits/earnings have you made?
    What pension provision have you made?
                    Total earned income

Investment income
    Self
    Spouse
    Do you or your spouse anticipate an increase or decrease in income?

Expenditure
    Mortgage details (if repayment type, principal plus interest)
    School fees
    Loans
    Any other liabilities

Mortgage type (i.e. Repayment, endowment, pension, etc.)
    If repayment, what are monthly payments (see above)?
    Amount of premiums on any mortgage protection policy
    If mortgage is pension or endowment mortgage, what is the amount of monthly interest?1
    What is the amount of monthly premiums on the endowment or pension portion?

SELLING LIFE ASSURANCE AND FINANCIAL PRODUCTS

When the mortgage commenced
Term remaining on mortgage
Outstanding amount

Retirement Provision:
Are you a member of your employer's pension scheme? YES/NO
When did you commence with your present employer?
What is the pension scheme retirement age?
Does the pension scheme provide for a capital sum and widow's pension on death before retirement? YES/NO
If YES, please give details.
Are you entitled to pension benefits from any previous employment? YES/NO
If self-employed, have you made or do you currently make any pension contributions (sec 226 plans or personal pension plan)? YES/NO
If YES, please give details of:
  (a) Which companies do you currently contribute to and how much?
  (b) Which companies have you made contributions to in the past and how much?
Have you any unused tax relief available to you in respect of the previous six tax years? YES/NO
If YES, please give details.
At what age do you intend to retire and take benefit?
Does your spouse have his or her own pension arrangement? YES/NO
If YES, please give details.
Please give details of any other relevant information not covered in the above sections of the questionnaire.

Short Factfind Checklist

For circumstances where it is more practical to work through a shorter checklist, here is a breakdown of the more important client details you should seek as part of your factfind.

1. Personal and family details: occupation, earned income, children, other dependants.
2. Assets, investments, investment income.
3. Liabilities: mortgage, school fees, other liabilities, e.g. personal loans, maintenance payments.
4. Pensions, life assurance, sickness and accident cover.
5. Wills, gifts made, inheritance expected and when.

6
Pointers to the Sale of Certain Products

The categories of financial product available range from variations on a theme to creatures different from one another in type and purpose. In this chapter we shall look at how best to present and sell some of the major types of product where they are indicated to be in the client's interests.

Life Assurance
Despite its somewhat sensitive reputation, the sale of life assurance for protection is not at all difficult if approached in the correct manner.

Life assurance must only be recommended where it is suited to a client's needs and can be set within the correct context of his or her financial affairs. It is the mindless flogging of life assurance policies by some unscrupulous salesmen without regard for a client's needs or wishes that has given its marketing a bad reputation. It is not enough to repeat the well-known maxim that 'life assurance is sold; it is never bought': it has to be sold to the right people at the right time. What is more, it is very readily bought by responsible and intelligent people who need it. It is the salesman's/consultant's job as a result of his factfinding and presentation to create a desire in the prospect's mind to buy what he needs. If life assurance is what the prospect needs, then life assurance is what should be sold.

There are some irrational people who simply will not buy life assurance, but they are few and will make no material difference to your sales ratio. What is more, even many of these can change their mind if approached in the proper manner and without appearing to push on your part. As for the rest, don't

SELLING LIFE ASSURANCE AND FINANCIAL PRODUCTS

waste your time or breath if you feel they lack the judgement to appreciate the merits of life assurance in their particular case. I remember an occasion some years ago when during a dinner one fellow guest I knew turned to me and said, 'I don't believe in life assurance.' I simply shrugged and replied, 'I suggest you check out that belief with your accountant or bank manager.' A few months later he got in touch with me and insisted he wanted the cheapest possible life assurance policy. After talking to his accountant and bank manager he realised that there was a gaping flaw in his financial affairs considering his responsibilities to the bank and his family. He was running a business on a large overdraft with the equity on his house as security. His only life assurance policy had been taken out to cover the much lower mortgage on his previous house at the insistence of the lender at that time. He had realised that life assurance had a rightful place in his affairs.

Before approaching the sale of life assurance (for protection) you must put yourself in the picture regarding the state of the prospect's financial affairs. You should find out how much life cover he has, in what form and whether he thinks it is sufficient. More often than not he will throw the question back at you and ask you what you think. You have stimulated his interest in the issue – a positive sign.

After analysing his position tell him honestly, slowly and looking him deliberately in the eye whether you think it is sufficient or not, concluding with the question, 'Would you agree?'

Your question will often prompt a friendly discussion of his requirements and you should arrive at an agreed conclusion. Do make sure that your prospect plays a full part in this discussion – do not monopolise it. Draw him out with questions like, 'When do you anticipate the children will be off your hands?' Brief and clear statements of fact such as 'Life assurance is dirt cheap especially if you are young, a non-smoker and don't need any money back while you are still alive. If you do want a return then we are moving into the realm of more sophisticated policies and you get what you pay for.' Point out your idea of the correct amount such as 'The aim should be to have a prudent amount such as a given multiple of your annual income. You shouldn't have unnecessary amounts of life assurance rammed down your throat. I can assure you that is not my intention.'

POINTERS TO THE SALE OF CERTAIN PRODUCTS

On the occasions when the prospect's life cover is grossly inadequate you can use, as I have often done, the following approach with great success. Turn silent for a few moments, and then say: 'Mr Jones, in terms of marketing life assurance you would be considered an A1 top of the list potential prospect. If one can't recommend and sell life assurance to someone in your position, who can one recommend it to?' Assuming you have correctly judged his sense of humour, it works very well. It works because you have led him to reflect upon his position and hopefully draw the correct conclusion.

Never fail to bring up the question of life assurance cover for wives. Always point out that they are even cheaper to insure than husbands. Point out with all the conviction you can command that this is a very important issue in view of the potential disruption to a husband's income and career if anything should happen to a young mother. I often ask, 'Would you like an idea of the cost?' and dip into my briefcase for my rate book. Husbands hardly ever refuse to insure wives with children when they realise the low cost. More often than not it is a case of looking at his wife, nodding mutual assent and saying, 'Yes, that seems a good idea; I think we'll go ahead with that.'

When explaining the features and benefits of life assurance policies it is useful to give the prospect a choice of alternatives between, say, a sophisticated and more expensive product and a cheaper and simpler one with more limited aims that still meet the prospect's needs. Giving this choice will sometimes increase your chances of a sale provided that you do not confuse the prospect with unnecessary detail which will defeat the object of the exercise and leave him undecided. For example, you may find some prospects who do not like the idea of simple term assurance without a return, while others are attracted to it because it is cheap and functional. The former will often approve of the more sophisticated unit-linked whole-of-life policy.

The type of life assurance policy and the amount of cover that you advocate must be dictated by the client's needs and requirements. His needs must be successfully brought home to him and the solution clearly illustrated in a manner that will create a desire to take up your recommendation. This correct identification of need and appropriate solution is essential if you are to retain long-term client confidence. To take a couple of examples, it may well be a correct recommendation for a middle-aged businessman to take up a whole-of-life policy for inheritance tax purposes. He may, after all, not yet have parted with any life-time gifts he may wish to make – and even if he has, there may be other gifts he may make later on. The potential inheritance tax liability can be expected to increase commensurate with a probable increase in the value of his assets. The policy can therefore be topped up and there is no cut-off date as in a term policy thus making it superfluous for inheritance tax purposes if he is alive at the end of the term and has not yet parted with any gifts. On the other hand, an elderly lady who has just made a gift of £100,000 needs a term policy for a period of seven years whose sum assured decreases simultaneously with inheritance tax liability regarding the gift over that seven-year period while still alive. This arrangement is the cheapest way of covering her potential liability. Such life policies taken out for inheritance tax purposes would normally be made out in trust, thus excluding its proceeds from the estate of the life assured. To sell her a whole-of-life policy would be extremely expensive for her as well as unnecessary.

Life assurance serves the interests of different people and for different purposes. It protects the estate of those fortunate to have a sizable estate. It creates an estate to pass on for those who don't. Provided that you present thoughtfully to those who have a need for it, concluding the sale should present no problems.

When assessing a prospect's life assurance position, look out, among others, for the following possible situations of necessity:

- Protecting a widow's (widower's) and/or other dependant's income.
- Ensuring full payment of a mortgage or other sizable loan.
- Creation of a fund for a specific purpose such as educating children, if death were to deprive the ability to fund for that purpose from the estate (possibly in trust for the benefit of specified beneficiaries).
- Inheritance tax planning.

POINTERS TO THE SALE OF CERTAIN PRODUCTS

The principal features and benefits of certain categories of life assurance with the primary aim of protective cover are set out below.

Level-term assurance
This is a cheap and straightforward life assurance that pays out a lump sum in the event of the death of the life assured within the preselected term. There is no surrender value and if the life assured survives until the end of the period specified the life assurance contract expires.

- It is very affordable. It can provide very high cover at low cost – extremely low cost for healthy young lives. It is even cheaper for females.
- Non-smokers' discount offers lower premiums for those who do not smoke. Some companies, however, have one rate for both smokers and non-smokers.
- It provides peace of mind.
- It ensures adequate financial security for one's dependants in the event of death, and enables the prospect's family to retain their independence and standard of living.
- The untimely death of a partner, before retirement, could result in financial insecurity for the surviving spouse. It therefore helps make up for reduced pension benefits in such cases.

Inflation-protected term assurance
This enables the level of protective cover (plus premiums) to increase in line with the Retail Price Index, without submitting further health evidence.

- It ensures that the real value of the protection granted to dependants is not eroded by inflation.

Mortgage protection (a decreasing term assurance)
The level of life assurance protection decreases according to the outstanding amount of mortgage. The cover takes into account upward variation in interest rates (even up to 20 per cent) and is costed accordingly.

- The peace of mind granted costs even less than level-term assurance.
- It ensures sufficient capital to pay off the outstanding mortgage in the event of the death of the life assured.
- It enables the assured's dependants to live in an unencumbered, fully paid home.

Convertible term assurance
This provides all the benefits of term assurance, but for a very small additional premium the policyholder:

- Has the option to keep extending his cover up to his 65th birthday, without submitting new evidence of health (regardless of the life assured's state of health).
- The policyholder may convert the policy to another term assurance, whole of life, endowment or other similar contract.
- The above features ensure that the policyholder need not worry about being unable to obtain cover in whatever format he or she chooses in the event of deterioration in health. The premiums, however, would be those applicable for the person's age at the time of conversion.

Family income benefit
This offers an alternative to providing a lump sum in the event of death.

- It pays a regular level of monthly tax-free income for the outstanding period of the plan in the event of the death of the life assured.
- It is especially useful for parents of young families where a monthly income is required to ensure payment of regular bills, school fees, mortgage, home help and other expenses.

Inflation protected family income benefit
Here the premiums as well as the benefits will rise in line with the Retail Price Index.

- In the event of the death of the life assured, it will ensure that the level of income of the dependants is not eroded by the effects of inflation.

POINTERS TO THE SALE OF CERTAIN PRODUCTS

Whole-of-life assurance
A fixed amount of money will be paid in the event of the death of the policyholder whenever it may occur. The premium is fixed.

- The policyholder knows that there will be no termination of the cover as long as he keeps on paying the premiums.
- It is useful for making provision for Inheritance Tax.

Whole-life with-profit policy
This ensures that bonuses are added to the sum assured each year.

- More useful for inheritance tax planning since the sum assured increases due to the addition of the bonuses, possibly making up for any increase in inheritance tax liability.
- The policy can usefully be converted to a finite-term endowment with profits to mature within the policyholder's lifetime, also taking into account all bonuses paid to date.

Unit-linked whole-of-life policy
This policy also lasts for the policyholder's lifetime and is a very flexible contract. In terms of the more usual contracts of this type I would present it to a prospect along the following lines.

Premiums are invested into a unit-linked fund of the client's choice. The life assurance cover can be chosen within very wide limits. A substantial level of life cover can be obtained at very reasonable cost, especially for younger lives.

It is designed to provide for a variable range of life assurance needs arising during the policyholder's lifetime. The chosen level of cover can be maintained for as long as the units in the underlying fund, into which the premiums are invested, grow at a minimum rate (usually) of 7.5 per cent. At the end of ten years there is a review. If the units have grown at the minimum rate required, the life cover may carry on at the original level for five more years and, subject to similar reviews at the end of each period, every five years thereafter up to about age 75, after which it would be reviewed annually. If the average annual growth rate of the fund has fallen below the minimum of, say, the required 7.5 per cent, the life assurance company will either request an increase in premium for the maintenance of the original level of cover, or ask the policyholder to take a lower level of cover.

Since the figure of 7.5 per cent is a conservative figure, the policyholder (or prospect) can have good reason to expect that the level of life cover chosen will continue for as long as he chooses. The policy can be surrendered with the surrender value dependent on the growth of the underlying fund.

If the policyholder at any time no longer requires the level of cover, he can reduce it to a level where the policy in effect becomes an investment policy with the reduced life cover a secondary matter.

The policy will normally contain an indexation option to enable the policyholder to increase either the life assurance cover (by an appropriate annual increase in contribution) or the contribution each year by a fixed percentage or in line with inflation. Usually, for a small additional payment, the contributions will be waived if the policyholder is unable to work for more than six months continuously due to illness or disability.

Policies of this type will usually contain some or all of the following additional features with the resulting potential benefits:

- For a small additional contribution the plan can incorporate accidental death benefit, which provides an additional payment (usually equal to the life assurance cover) where death is caused by accident. This is an inexpensive way of boosting the life assurance protection of the prospect to cope with sudden unexpected death.
- Without further evidence of health, the policyholder has the option to effect an additional plan upon the birth or legal adoption of a child.
- Redundancy benefit: where available, this will allow contributions to be missed for up to six months due to redundancy. If the benefit is taken, contributions can be restarted at a later date at which time the life assurance cover will then be reviewed. There is normally no extra

contribution for this benefit and it may normally be taken up twice in ten years, subject to certain limits.
- If the life cover is reduced at any time, then provided contributions have been maintained a replacement may be effected without further health evidence being required. Usually the life cover on a new plan must not exceed the reduction in the level of life cover minus any cash value taken out at the time.

This type of policy is very useful and valuable and therefore saleable, particularly to a young working man with a young family, or intending to start one. The principal overall benefit to emphasise, after reviewing the plan along the above lines, is that he could take care of a substantial portion of his life assurance needs for a long time, especially if he were to incorporate an indexation option. He would be doing so at extremely good value too, due to the surrender value that the policy will be building up in addition to providing good life cover. In fact, the surrender value could eventually make the policy exceptionally good value if the underlying fund grows at a good rate. It should be pointed out that this will not in itself make the policy an investment as such unless and until he actually reduces the life cover to the level where the investment aspect of the policy takes precedence, by the contributions being invested with only a tiny fraction paying for life cover.

It should be stressed to the prospect that ultimately, if and when he no longer requires the policy, he can surrender it and receive the full surrender value.

Critical illness insurance
This type of insurance is being offered by an increasing number of insurance companies and is justifiably gaining an increasing market. It offers a most valuable financial protection and relief against a potentially distressing situation. It is designed to provide a guaranteed lump sum in the event of a person being diagnosed as suffering from a critical illness.

The contract stipulates that a guaranteed cash sum will be paid following a specified survival time span of, say, fifteen days after diagnosis of a specified critical illness. The cover will continue up to a specified age, usually 60. The range of illnesses covered can vary among insurance companies but generally includes most or all of the following: heart attack, cancer (except certain skin cancers), stroke, coronary artery disease requiring surgery, kidney failure, major organ transplant, paraplegia, heart valve surgery, paralysis or loss of two or more limbs, permanent blindness in both eyes, AIDS through blood transfusion in the UK, complete disability arising from the later stages of disease such as multiple sclerosis or rheumatoid arthritis. In at least one contract I have examined, it states that benefits may still be paid if a policyholder suffers a serious illness or accident prior to age 60 which leaves him or her totally and irreversibly disabled even though the claim would not satisfy the definitions of any of the specific illnesses covered. Permanent total disability cover continues while the plan is in force but ceases on the policyholder's 60th birthday.

With most, but not all, companies offering this cover, it is provided as an addition to a life assurance policy, such as term assurance, mortgage endowment type policy or unit linked whole of life. In the event of a claim under the critical illness insurance segment, the principal policy will either cease or the sum assured will be reduced by the amount already paid to the insured person under the critical illness insurance.

Apart from its own intrinsic value, it can provide the prospect with added motivation to take out life assurance. It can and is mostly sold as additional protection to complement an appropriate life assurance policy, thus extending the range of protection and consequent peace of mind. The latter point is the most important one to emphasise to a prospect. You can point out that should such an unfortunate situation arise it can enable a policyholder to (1) avoid dipping into savings for expenses such as paying for the best possible treatment or transport adaptation, (2) pay off the mortgage if required, and (3) not have to worry about money.

Don't try and sell this insurance by being alarmist. Most people have enough sense to appreciate the value of this type of insurance if you explain it simply and accurately. You need to know and point out clearly any additional useful features the particular brand name policy you want to sell may contain, such as inflation proofing and waiver of premium.

POINTERS TO THE SALE OF CERTAIN PRODUCTS

The important message you need to convey is the benefit of peace of mind and protection. This is what we life assurance salespeople have to impart to our clients: to make their lives more content, more free of worry. If you occasionally feel like spelling this out to them, do so. It is fair comment – and should also reassure them.

In addition to the benefits of life assurance already listed you should bear in mind its uses for the purposes of business planning and inheritance tax mitigation. Below are three practical and important uses of life assurance – and consequently possible selling opportunities – that you should look out for. However, advising in these situations can be complex, and you should not attempt to do so before you have undertaken the appropriate study and training, as well as refresher and updating courses as and when necessary.

Partnership insurance (including share purchase insurance)
The purpose of partnership (or share purchase) insurance is to help provide funds with which the surviving partners of a deceased person can buy his or her share of a partnership, or help surviving shareholders of a private limited company to buy a deceased shareholder's holding. This can have the following benefits.

- By providing funds it prevents the need to borrow, to liquidate assets or to use badly needed funds in order to buy the deceased person's share.
- It removes the need to find new partners or shareholders with capital, or to involve the deceased's widow(er) in the business.
- The deceased person's dependants or those otherwise entitled to his or her estate can benefit immediately from the sale of the deceased's stake in the business.

This is a topic that should be very much in your mind during contacts with company directors and other businesspeople, or professionals in partnerships such as architects or solicitors.

Keyman insurance
This will compensate an employer for the loss of profits arising from the death of a key employee. Look out therefore for situations where:

- The employer has provided all or most of the capital for the enterprise, but the keyman has the technical knowhow that keeps the business running.
- Situations where the keyman is important because of his special connections with, say, a given market. For example, a British manufacturing employer's keyman may be someone with detailed knowledge of and connections with vital Middle Eastern or South American markets.
- Any other situation where the loss of a keyman's services would result in financial loss or prove difficult or expensive to replace.

It is important to point out to a prospect that the premiums payable are allowed as a business expense provided that:

- The sole relationship of the life assured to the company is that of an employer to an employee.
- The life assurance is for the purpose of covering loss of profits arising from the loss of the keyman's services.
- The policy is a short-term assurance, normally not exceeding five years (in exceptional circumstances, however, up to ten years or more may be acceptable).

You should note that if the premiums are allowed as a business expense against corporation tax, the proceeds of the insurance when received will be taxed as income of the company. This should be taken into consideration when determining the sum assured. For this reason, and due to other possible tax implications, you need to study the topic in depth before you give advice.

It should be pointed out that it is also possible to insure against the disablement of a key employee.

POINTERS TO THE SALE OF CERTAIN PRODUCTS

Inheritance tax mitigation

A life assurance policy can be written under trust for the benefit of nominated beneficiaries for the purpose of funding for (or mitigating) inheritance tax. The precise type of policy to be used will depend upon the circumstances.

For example, the appropriate policy indicated if death should occur within seven years of a potentially exempt transfer would be a seven-year term assurance that decreases according to what tax would be payable in the event of the death of the life assured. On the other hand, a whole-life policy could be used to meet inheritance tax payable on the death of a surviving spouse. An appropriate arrangement would be for such a whole-life policy to be written on a joint life, last survivor basis.

Due to the varying individual circumstances that may arise careful planning is required for the funding of inheritance tax, and you should not attempt to advise on this topic unless and until you have received the appropriate training and therefore have the authority of your employers or principals to do so. My purpose in bringing it to your attention here is simply to emphasise that you should be aware of the sales possibilities if you have the appropriate training and authority. It is not an attempt to impart the required technical knowledge.

Pensions

The radical changes in pension legislation that came into effect in 1988 have created new and unsurpassed opportunities for members of our profession. Pension planning and advice is now a major source of commission income.

The issue of pensions is far too important a part of an individual's financial planning to ignore or even to gloss over. You should always obtain the full facts relating to a prospect's pension position and keep your existing clients' records up to date in this respect. The subject should be raised as a separate item on all occasions that you contact the prospect, especially where you suspect that there may be scope for discussing the issue in depth at your meeting.

When you phone a prospect you should ask him to give you an idea of his pension situation. A brief outline by him of his

SELLING LIFE ASSURANCE AND FINANCIAL PRODUCTS

position plus a few probing questions by yourself will enable you to spot any opportunities for improving his situation, with resulting business for yourself. This can range from a new personal pension plan, an increase in contributions to an existing one, an executive pension plan, and free-standing additional voluntary contributions to possible transfer plans of previous pension benefits. In such situations you should ask the prospect to agree to a discussion without any obligation.

If a prospect informs you, or if you already know from your records, that he already has a pension scheme with his employer simply ask him if he is 'making full pension contributions'. The average teacher or local government employee, for example, contributes 6 per cent of his or her salary, leaving up to a further 9 per cent that can go into additional free-standing voluntary contributions. It will help you to have prior knowledge of the pension schemes of a variety of employers and professions. When you bring up the subject on the phone, for example, you can say, 'My information is, Mr Jones, that as a local government employee you are paying 6 per cent of your income into your superannuation.' He will immediately be alerted to the fact that you are speaking with knowledge and authority relating to his particular pension situation. You can go on, 'This leaves you with up to a further 9 per cent of your income which you can contribute towards your pension in the form of additional voluntary contributions. The subject is too complex to discuss over the phone. May I suggest we meet. I promise I'll give you a complete and clear picture of the situation and your opportunities. You are, of course, under no obligation.'

Whenever you secure an appointment always ascertain the prospect's date of birth if you don't already know it. This will enable you to arrive at your meeting armed with illustrative quotes. I suggest that you also obtain for comparison – in addition to the principal quote based on his date of birth – one set of quotes based on that of an individual exactly one year older and a third based on someone exactly a year younger. This will forcefully illustrate the disparity in his prospective pension, even at the modest rate of return allowed under LAUTRO rules, between starting a given monthly/annual contribution now and deferring commencement for a year. The

POINTERS TO THE SALE OF CERTAIN PRODUCTS

third set of quotes will further drive home the point by illustrating how much better off he would have been had he started those contributions last year. Indeed, you will often be surprised yourself at the disparity in ultimate benefits. It costs nothing after all to obtain these quotes.

All that is necessary for a successful sale is a clear explanation of how a given scheme works, what benefits can be expected, clear honest answers to questions (which are buying signals) and an assurance of the good record and reputation of the pension company involved. When it comes to explaining complex products such as pensions and free-standing AVCs, it is helpful to make your own notes of a product's features and benefits in logical order and practise explaining them to yourself aloud. A method I have found useful is to take the literature available on a product and underline the key passages in red. These then form the framework of your explanation. It will also help the client's own permanent retention of the facts when he reads the literature and finds that it corresponds to the order in which you outlined it.

You will therefore successfully convey your recommendations if you explain and illustrate the main features and emphasise the principal benefits of a plan that meets the prospect's needs. You should strengthen your case by pointing out any specially attractive features with special benefits peculiar to that particular product or brand – i.e. the unique selling points.

Below are the main features and benefits that you should convey to a prospect for each of the main types of pension product. They are not intended to be a detailed exposition of each product. Do remember therefore to expand upon and emphasise where necessary the benefits of special interest to a particular prospect's needs, and with the degree of detail required.

Personal pension plan for employees
This provides an efficiently planned income in retirement which can be taken at any time between ages 50 and 75, regardless of whether the prospect is still working or not. It is in addition to a contracted-out SERPS or a contracted-out arrangement, whereby the DSS will redirect into a personal pension plan that part of the National Insurance Contributions which would have provided the State Earnings-Related Pension Scheme.

- The prospect and employer combined can contribute up to 17.5 per cent of net relevant earnings or the higher limit, depending on age.
- Income tax relief on contributions at the highest rate of tax that the prospect pays. Do mention to the prospect that although contributions are paid net after basic rate income tax relief, higher-rate taxpayers receive a certificate enabling them to reclaim additional contributions through their tax assessment.
- The prospect's contributions are invested in funds which grow without being subject to income tax, corporation tax or capital gains tax. This means greater growth of the underlying fund, resulting in the highest possible commensurate pension.
- The prospect can take up to 25 per cent of the accumulated fund as a tax-free lump sum on retirement.
- There is flexibility in the prospect's chosen level of contributions. The prospect can increase, decrease or suspend payments as he feels necessary.
- It is possible to take part of the benefits upon retiring early and postpone the balance of payments until later.
- The plan is fully portable. The prospect can move the plan from job to job. The great advantage here is that he can continue paying contributions under one plan until retirement.
- The prospect has the option to transfer the accumulated fund to another pension provider, if he can get a better pension at the time that he decides to draw his pension.
- The prospect can use the tax-free cash element of the fund to pay off a pension mortgage. He also has the option of taking a loanback while still working.
- Do assure the prospect that should he die before retirement, the full value of the plan will be paid to the prospect's estate or to secure pension benefits for the person or persons nominated in trust to enable payment to be made by the trustees without waiting for probate.
- Additional life assurance can be added to the pension plan to provide extra protection for dependants. The premiums for this attract full tax relief and he can contribute up to 5 per cent of his net relevant earnings.

POINTERS TO THE SALE OF CERTAIN PRODUCTS

Point out that this 5 per cent limit is inclusive of the overall percentage that can be contributed to a personal pension plan.
- For a small additional premium of about 3 per cent of the regular premium, the prospect can protect his pension in the event of being unable to maintain premiums due to illness or injury. In such an event the contributions are automatically maintained until the prospect is able to start work again or may continue until retirement age.
- The prospect has total control over the nature and investment philosophy of the funds into which the contributions are invested, as well as being able to decide how and in what proportion contributions are to be allocated. He can play safe, for example, and choose a managed or with profits fund (if available).
- The prospect can change the balance of the fund investments at any time, thus allowing him to play an active part in his pension investments. Point out that the first such switching facility in each year will (usually) be free.
- Assuming it to be the case, stress the security and peace of mind arising from the knowledge that the plan you are recommending is backed and managed by a leading life assurance society (or other financial institution) with many years' experience in meeting people's financial needs.
- Emphasise any unique features and resulting benefits that the plan may have that give it an edge over other competing plans. These can be powerful selling points.

Point out that the prospect will be able to keep track of the fortunes of his pension fund. He will receive a statement at least once a year illustrating the correct value of his accumulated contributions and a projection of the position at retirement. In addition, he will be able to follow the prices of units in which the fund may be invested (if indeed it is a unit fund) in the leading newspapers.

Where appropriate you should emphasise that the sooner the prospect starts to contribute towards a pension, the more the pension builds up.

SELLING LIFE ASSURANCE AND FINANCIAL PRODUCTS

Self-employed personal pension plan
You are no doubt aware that the features and benefits of a personal pension plan for the self-employed are in most respects identical to those for an employed person. There are, however, a number of points specific to a self-employed plan with features and benefits that should be pointed out.

- This is the only fully tax efficient pension plan that the self-employed prospect who has not incorporated his business (see executive pension plan) can, and indeed should take out, if he wishes to maintain his financial security in retirement. The plan is as flexible and as tax efficient as any pension scheme. The only other pension available to the self-employed individual who has not made retirement provision is the basic state pension, which by itself won't get him very far. He cannot even look forward to a State Earnings-Related Pension on top of the basic State Pension, as can a contracted-in employee who has no occupational scheme.
- The prospect can choose to retire at any time between the ages of 50 and 75, unless he is in the type of occupation where he can, with Inland Revenue permission, retire earlier, such as a jockey.
- The prospect will be able to reduce his income tax burden by receiving tax relief on his contributions at the highest rate of tax he pays. You should point out to the prospect, however, that these contributions are paid gross and that he claims the tax relief through his tax assessment.
- The prospect can make extra contributions to his pension plan to sweep up unused tax relief he may have left over from any one or more of the previous six years.
- The percentage of his net relevant earnings that the prospect can contribute to his plan are subject to an upper earnings limit of £75,000 for 1992/93 tax year (as for employees), increasing in subsequent years in line with increases to the Retail Price Index. You will in practice find few people who will be able to contribute this sort of upper limit amount.
- The prospect can contribute up to 17.5 per cent of his net relevant earnings towards his pension scheme, or up to

POINTERS TO THE SALE OF CERTAIN PRODUCTS

- the higher limits that apply to those aged over 35.
- The plan is flexible and if the prospect were to become employed it remains in force (subject to eligibility) except that the contributions would then be paid net of basic rate income tax.
- As in the case of an employed person's personal pension plan, single lump sum payments can be made at any time. This is particularly important in the case of a self-employed individual who may not be sure of his total earnings until towards the end of the tax year. He may then feel in a position to make a lump sum contribution in addition to his regular monthly contributions.
- As in the case of an employed person, he may take out additional life assurance within the plan and receive full tax relief on the cost of the premiums (together with those of pension contributions). Furthermore, for a small additional premium – which will also attract tax relief – he can protect his retirement benefits in the event of being unable to work due to injury or long illness. In such an event his contributions will be automatically maintained until he has recovered sufficiently to be able to work again.
- The plan will give him even greater security and peace of mind by the knowledge that he does not have to rely for his retirement income on the continuing prosperity and the sale of the business when he retires.
- The prospect can take out a pension mortgage whereby the loan is repaid from the tax-free cash element of the pension plan. Whether he takes up a pension mortgage or not, do point out that he is entitled to take up to 25 per cent of the accumulated pension fund as a tax-free lump sum.
- In addition to a pension mortgage the prospect may have the option to take out a loanback.
- The prospect may take pension benefits and continue working if he wishes. He can also plan his retirement and take his benefit in stages.

You should take every opportunity to bring up the subject of pensions with any self-employed individual who is a potential prospect. You will be surprised at the number of people who have yet to do anything at all about their pension, or whose current contributions are far below what they can and should contribute. They will usually be grateful to you for raising the issue.

Free-standing additional voluntary contribution plans (FSAVC)
The marketing of FSAVC Plans constitutes one of the most potentially rewarding opportunities open to financial consultants: they are particularly useful and beneficial to eligible members of the working population. In numerical terms you may even find yourself selling more of these plans than personal pension plans or executive pension plans (dealt with below).

Provided a prospect is eligible and there is scope for an FSAVC Plan in addition to his occupational scheme, you will often find that he has in principle made up his mind to go ahead before you have actually finished your presentation. Again, do make sure that you are familiar with the technical specifications of the plan so that you are able to present accurately and answer any queries that may arise.

You should start your presentation by reminding the prospect that he is currently either not contributing towards his main occupational pension scheme or contributing a small set percentage of his gross income, thus leaving him with the balance percentage figure of up to 15 per cent which he may contribute into an FSAVC Plan. The main points that you need to convey and impress upon prospects relating to FSAVC Schemes are as follows:

- The FSAVC Plan is an excellent tax-advantageous means of boosting the retirement income that will emanate from the main occupational scheme, up to the maximum permitted by the Inland Revenue (refer to technical specifications for Inland Revenue limits), without suffering loss to the benefits provided by the employer's pension scheme.
- Emphasise that in addition to the benefits that the prospect will receive from his employer's pension scheme, he will also receive a pension as a result of

POINTERS TO THE SALE OF CERTAIN PRODUCTS

contributions to this plan. He will receive the additional benefits at the same time as his main scheme benefits or later if he wishes, but not earlier. The prospect will thus ensure that he has made use of the maximum opportunity available to him to enjoy the best possible permitted pension.
- A particularly useful benefit of an FSAVC is that it will allow the prospect to take the maximum tax-free cash sum from the occupational scheme at retirement and use the FSAVC to replace that portion of the pension that he has given up in exchange for the cash sum (subject to total benefits not exceeding Inland Revenue limits).
- The prospect may contribute to this plan even if he is a member of a company AVC scheme.
- The prospect will receive tax relief at the top rate of tax he pays. His contributions will be paid net of basic rate tax. If he is a higher-rate tax payer he receives a certificate enabling him to reclaim the additional tax relief on his contributions. Make the point also that the savings are substantial, as in effect the taxman is paying his contributions for him.
- Contributions are invested in funds which grow without being subject to income tax, corporation tax or capital gains tax, thus taking advantage of greater potential capital growth.
- The prospect may choose when and how much he contributes. He can increase, decrease or suspend them to suit his circumstances. He can also make single lump sum payments during the year. He can thus take advantage of any sums he may receive, such as for overtime, commission, bonus or profit sharing.
- The plan is fully portable. He can take it with him whenever he changes jobs. He can thus continue paying contributions into his FSAVC while also accruing benefits in his new employer's pension scheme.
- An FSAVC Plan is particularly useful if the prospect wishes to fund for early retirement.
- At pension time the prospect may transfer his accumulated pension fund to another (authorised) pension provider if offered more favourable terms. He may also,

provided the trustees of the employees pension scheme agree, transfer his FSAVC retirement fund to his employer's scheme enabling all benefits to be paid from the same source.
- Note that the prospect cannot by law contribute to more than one FSAVC arrangement in respect of the same employment in any tax year. Therefore if the prospect is already making FSAVC contributions to another plan in respect of the same employment and wishes to invest in another plan (such as the one you may be recommending) instead, he may do so from the beginning of the following tax year, provided contributions to the other FSAVC cease.
- The prospect will have complete freedom of choice as to where additional contributions are invested, by being able to choose among a range of funds. He will therefore not be restricted to the type of option normally available to in-house AVCs. He can also defer drawing a pension arising from an FSAVC, till well after he starts drawing his employer's pension. This will allow the fund to build up and result in a larger pension.
- The sooner the prospect starts additional contributions, the more his pension will build up. Even a year's delay will have a significant effect upon the ultimate benefits. Illustrate this with quotes.
- The prospect will have the security and peace of mind arising from the fact that his plan will be backed and managed by a leading institution with years of experience in providing for people's financial requirements (which is the sort of institution whose product you should be recommending).

As I mentioned earlier regarding presentations, do ensure that you control the interview. You should ensure that each point you make sinks in and any queries are dealt with to the prospect's satisfaction, before you go on to the next point.

I suggest that you always have a pension manual handy in order to confirm and expand where necessary on any information you impart, as well as to enable you to reinforce a point you may wish to drive home.

POINTERS TO THE SALE OF CERTAIN PRODUCTS

Pension transfer plans (to personal pension plan)
There are many opportunities for the arrangement of transfer plans from a deferred pension fund that are appropriate, and in the interest of relevant prospects. It is for you to assess, after gathering the relevant data, which deferred pensions are appropriate for transfer and on balance better for the prospect, and which ones are better off remaining where they are. Only if you deem it better for your prospect should you advocate a transfer of the deferred pension. There are many people who have pension benefits remaining with one or more former employers' occupational pension schemes.

There are very good reasons for transferring a deferred pension, where suitable, to a personal pension. Although some 'frozen' pensions may receive increases to offset the effects of inflation, these pensions can now be unlocked and transferred to a personal pension plan, enabling the prospect to exercise investment control and take advantage of the opportunity to benefit by improving his pension significantly.

Take the opportunity of inquiring from every prospect, certainly during your factfind, but also when you spot an opportunity with a potential prospect, whether he or she has any pension benefits remaining with a former employer. This topic also provides an opportunity for the last throw technique described in the chapter on prospecting. If a prospect does have frozen pension benefits that in your judgement are likely to benefit by being transferred to a personal pension plan, you should point out and emphasise the features and benefits listed below. However, you should advise a transfer only after gathering all the relevant information and after comparing the possible benefits of a personal pension plan or Section 32 Bond to the potential benefits of the previous pension scheme (this comparative analysis is dealt with below). It is important to bear in mind and point out that even if the prospect is currently in an employer's occupational pension scheme, he can still transfer his deferred previous pension benefits to a personal pension plan, to which he could not, of course, make further regular contributions while in the current employer's scheme.

- The transfer value and subsequent benefits are fully entitled to the complete favourable tax treatment of any

pension scheme. The transfer values are invested in funds which like all pension funds grow free of UK investment income and capital gains tax. The prospect may take part of the retirement benefits in the form of a tax-free lump sum.
- The prospect may carry on paying regular contributions into the fund, if he is not currently in an occupational scheme, and receive tax relief at his top rate of tax.
- If the prospect's previous company scheme was contracted out of SERPS, the replacement benefits can be transferred to this plan to secure Protected Rights benefits. These SERPS replacement benefits could (and in my opinion are likely to) be substantially increased by the investment growth of the fund(s) chosen.
- The prospect can exercise control by choosing from a range of funds to suit his investment requirements, ranging from a high degree of security to high but potentially more lucrative degrees of risk.
- In the case of many plans it is possible, within limits, for the prospect to exercise even greater control and flexibility by nominating an investment manager (other than the product company's investment managers) and being involved in the asset selection and establishment of a personal portfolio to suit his requirements. It thus combines the advantages of an insured pension contract with facilities to the policyholder of exercising control over investment strategy.
- As with any personal pension scheme the plan gives the prospect a choice of when to take benefits at any time between 50 and 75, or to phase the benefits over a period of time. Any SERPS replacement benefits, however, cannot be taken before age 65 for males and age 60 for females.
- The prospect retains full control over his benefit rights, especially if circumstances change. He can also transfer the value of the plan to another authorised pension provider, be it to a new employer's occupational pension scheme (subject to the agreement of the trustees of the new scheme) or to another personal pension plan.
- There is family protection, because on death before retirement the value of the investments will be available

POINTERS TO THE SALE OF CERTAIN PRODUCTS

to secure benefits. Normally 25 per cent of the pension fund will be payable as a lump sum and the balance used to secure a pension for the spouse.

The above is purely a summary of the key features and resulting benefits intended to be conveyed during your presentation. Do make sure that you have a sufficient overall knowledge of the plan in order to deal satisfactorily with any reasonable queries that may be thrown at you.

Section 32 buyout bonds
The case for taking out one of these is similar to that of transferring frozen pension benefits with a former employer to a personal pension as described above. For younger employees transfer to a personal pension will usually be more advantageous than a buyout bond. Bear in mind also that these are single contribution plans purchased at the request of the member by the trustees of an occupational pension scheme (who must be a party to the contract) in the name of the member who has left pensionable employment.

It should be pointed out that if the former employer's scheme was contracted out, a Section 32 buyout plan can accept the Guaranteed Minimum Pension liability (in respect of the Social Security Pensions Act 1975), thus ensuring that the prospect member will receive at least as much as the Guaranteed Minimum Pension provided by the prospect's former pension scheme. The pension providing institution will therefore need to provide at least the Guaranteed Minimum Pension.

Point out that the Section 32 buyout plan must provide benefits within the Inland Revenue limits, and will normally match the paid up pension of the employer that the prospect is leaving. There is also the possibility that it will provide higher benefits if the pension rights are transferred to a well chosen with-profits or unit-linked fund.

Matters relating to the transfer decision
Before your prospect decides on whether to transfer or not, to enable you to give sound advice you will need to obtain a letter from him authorising and requesting the trustees of his

SELLING LIFE ASSURANCE AND FINANCIAL PRODUCTS

previous pension scheme to give your firm and yourself all the relevant information that you will need relating to that scheme. You will then have to write to the trustees, enclosing the prospect's letter of authority to them, and request all the necessary information, including that required to make a comparison. You must then obtain illustrative quotations from the product company to aid you in advising the prospect as to whether he should transfer or not.

An efficient way to go about this is as follows:

- With the aid of the quotes that illustrate the rates of return earned on the transfer value, compare the pension that your prospect can receive from the previous pension scheme with what he or she might receive from a personal pension plan or a Section 32 buyout bond.
- Compare the tax-free cash available under the company scheme, a personal pension, and a Section 32 bond, including the limits allowed under such a bond. Transfers to a Section 32 plan effected on or after the 29 November 1991 would qualify for automatic indexation of the tax-free cash entitlement, in line with increases in RPI, from the date of leaving to the date of taking benefits. (Note that under a transfer to a personal pension plan, the tax-free cash at retirement is restricted to 25 per cent of the fund or a certified amount times RPI if lower.)
- Compare the rates of return that must be earned on the transfer value to equal the scheme benefits, if the prospective client transfers out.

At least one company that I know of (National Provident Institution) is most helpful in this respect and has introduced a Pensions Transfer Analysis Service which includes an information package that enables one to make the above comparisons and also indicates if the client should consider opting for the post-1989 Finance Act regime; this may lead to an increase in the tax-free cash available at retirement. The package includes a data request form for the trustees to complete with the information necessary to produce a comparison illustration. It is worth noting, however, that if there is any difficulty getting such a form completed, a copy of your client's leaver statement is

POINTERS TO THE SALE OF CERTAIN PRODUCTS

usually sufficient. To assist consultants an increasing number of institutions are bringing out good transfer analysis packages and software systems to assess whether transferring out of a company scheme is viable and to be recommended.

You should consider all the information before you make a considered judgement and give the appropriate advice. In this respect, independent financial advisers and their appointed registered representatives should take note of and abide by FIMBRA's guidelines (Guidance Note No.7, reproduced below) on the key factors that should be considered when dealing with possible pension transfers from a final salary scheme. Similar guidance has been issued by LAUTRO in their Enforcement Bulletin No. 16. Also, the SIB has proposed that from July 1994 all pension transfer analysis be carried out on computer software.

FIMBRA Guidance Note No. 7

TRANSFERS FROM FINAL SALARY PENSION SCHEMES

FIMBRA is concerned that beneficiaries under final salary pension schemes may be disadvantaged when receiving advice on transfer options. Valuable benefits can be lost on a transfer.

This Guidance Note sets out the practice members should follow when dealing with this type of business.

1. Rights under the final salary scheme
   It should be clearly demonstrated that the beneficiaries' rights in the scheme are fully taken into account. Items such as:

   (a) guaranteed pension at retirement;
   (b) spouses' and children's pensions;
   (c) indexation of pensions in payment both guaranteed and discretionary;
   (d) guarantees under GMPs;
   (e) statutory indexation of preserved benefits and the history of discretionary increases provided;
   (f) risk benefits payable on death or long term disability or illness;
   (g) the 'transfer club' rights applicable for members of public sector schemes;
   (h) the beneficiaries' age and attitude to investment risk;

SELLING LIFE ASSURANCE AND FINANCIAL PRODUCTS

  (i) the potential for loss on moving from 'uncapped' final salary benefits to 'capped' personal pensions for pre-1989 scheme beneficiaries;
  (j) the prospect of the final salary scheme benefits increasing further as a result of:
   (i) the limited price indexation and surplus provisions of the Social Security Act 1990 coming into force; and
   (ii) the resolution of the Barber vs. GRE case on equal retirement ages;
  (k) the view taken on the financial security of the pension scheme, for example by reference to the Trustees' Report and Accounts and also the composition of the Board of Trustees;

 need to be considered and discussed with the client.

2. Advising on the options
 There are four main options:

  (a) leave deferred benefits in the final salary scheme or remain in scheme membership if not leaving service;
  (b) transfer to a new employer's scheme;
  (c) transfer to a personal pension plan;
  (d) transfer to a Section 32 policy.

 An analysis of the value of the deferred benefits and a comparison of the alternatives is essential; this will take into account investment risk and performance and, also, initial and ongoing charges. It is expected many cases will lead to the correct advice being option (a), i.e. final salary scheme or remain in scheme membership if not leaving service. Indeed, for those remaining in service, option (a) should be assumed to be correct as future prospective benefits, not just past service benefits, are at risk. This particularly applies to public sector schemes because of inflation guarantees and the 'transfer club'. Any transfer out should be carefully justified in detail.

3. Records

 The client file should demonstrate that the three transfer options (b), (c) and (d) have been considered. Attention should be paid to details of the transfer alternatives. Members' files should show why a particular option was selected, especially where that option meant:

  (a) the loss of guaranteed rights;
  (b) the choice of either a Section 32 contract or a personal pension plan.

4. Similar guidance is being issued by LAUTRO.

POINTERS TO THE SALE OF CERTAIN PRODUCTS

Group personal pension schemes
A group personal pension scheme is cost-effective, tax-advantageous, and also the simplest way that an employer prospect can enable employees to provide for their retirement.

It will be in the interest of many employees to contract out of SERPS to make them eligible to claim National Insurance rebates in respect of their own and their employer's National Insurance contributions. However, since the government wants to reduce public expenditure, it is possible that it will eventually transfer the administration of National Insurance rebates to employers instead of through the DSS. The point needs to be made, therefore, that by acting now the prospect as an employer can avoid being faced with future administration problems of this nature. He could be faced with the difficult administrative problem of making regular contributions to many different pension providers for different respective employees. This potential problem can be easily avoided by offering and providing a group personal pension plan, administered by a respected pension provider with its easy and simple contribution collecting facility. The employer can then remit all his contributions (if any) and those of his employees via one direct debit mandate.

By offering and contributing to his employees' pension plan, the prospect can attract and keep the employees he wants and thus gain an advantage over his competitors. This would constitute a significant incentive to employees weighing up their overall employment benefits.

- All contributions made by the prospect employer will normally be treated as an expense against profits and be eligible for full tax relief.
- The employer's contributions would not increase the employees' payroll (which would be liable for National Insurance). This creates a further saving when compared to a straightforward salary increase.
- The employees are allowed to contribute up to 17.5 per cent of their net annual earnings, inclusive of any contributions made by the employer. For those over 35, quote the appropriate percentages of net relevant earnings.
- Employees' contributions are paid net of basic rate tax,

but employers' contributions are paid gross. Employees will receive a certificate enabling higher-rate tax payers to obtain the extra tax relief through their assessment.
- Any contracted-out contributions received from the DSS will include a basic rate income tax refund on their portion of the National Insurance rebate.
- All contributions are invested in funds that grow free of income tax, corporation tax and capital gains tax, thus enabling greater growth.
- A group personal pension plan will help safeguard the future of employees by providing:

  (a) A pension at ages 50 to 75.
  (b) A tax-free lump sum.
  (c) Inflation proofing if desired by being made to increase each year.
  (d) Benefits on death before retirement, by being provided from the accumulated value of the fund.
  (e) Benefits on death after retirement in the form of widow's or widower's pension.
  (f) Additional life assurance if desired.

- Even if the employer does not contribute now, the plan offers the facility to contribute at any time in the future.
- Contributions can be paid monthly or yearly. Single one-off payments may be made at any time. The employer can keep up with the changing circumstances or maximise tax advantages by being able to increase, decrease or even suspend payments.
- Employees can exercise a degree of control over their pension by being able to choose from a range of funds. They can also switch their investments or the balance of investments between different funds.
- The employer prospect can thus help employees make a good investment decision regarding their pension, which will be backed and managed by a good company with long experience of looking after people's financial needs and investments,
- The plan is flexible, as encouraged by legislation. Contributions can be collected from employers only,

POINTERS TO THE SALE OF CERTAIN PRODUCTS

employees only or both. They can be collected on behalf of some or all of the employees. In addition, each employee is free to transfer his share of the accumulated fund to another pension provider at any time.

Executive pension plans (director's pension)
Directors of private companies often delay arranging a tax efficient retirement scheme. This may be due to a sense of security engendered by the notion that the business after all represents the security he has worked so hard for, and that some day he will simply sell it and then invest and live off the proceeds. He may also think that he will pass over the business to his children and reach an arrangement with them whereby he draws an income from the company.

If any of these arguments are advanced – which is quite possible among the less financially sophisticated of company directors – it is essential that you deal with these issues before you list the benefits of the scheme. You should make the point that if he is relying on selling the business when he retires for his future income, he may not be in the strongest position to do so at the time when he needs the money. He may risk having to sell it for a lower price than if he were in a position to wait for a higher price. Even more important, the vagaries of the business market are such that the fact of having a successful business today is no guarantee that he will have a particularly successful or sought-after business to sell later.

When it comes to stating your case for the prospect taking out an executive pension plan for himself and key employees, it is important that among the numerous benefits you lay special stress on the tax advantages, including the fact that it is a far more advantageous method than any other of ensuring an income in retirement from the business itself. When presenting plans such as this, I recommend that you have with you an appropriate impartial manual, preferably aimed at the layman, to which you can turn for support and which will back up the tax and other benefits of taking up a scheme such as this. A particularly suitable publication for pension purposes is that by Tony Reardon entitled *Planning your Pension* (published by Longman with Allied Dunbar). It is worth emphasising that taking money out of a company any other way to provide and

SELLING LIFE ASSURANCE AND FINANCIAL PRODUCTS

build up funds for retirement is likely to come up against the Inland Revenue's insistence on its cut. Given the fact that with an executive pension plan you have, apart from all the other advantages, a perfectly legitimate method of reducing corporation tax and directly benefiting one's key employees, this represents an ideal vehicle for planning the prospect director's and his employees' retirement income.

The main features and benefits of taking out an executive pension plan that should be conveyed to a suitable prospect are listed below. You don't have to reel them off in this order or detail; you can convey the most important and relevant, and weave in the others according to the pattern of your presentation and the resulting discussion. The order in which they are set out, however, is logical.

- It is a pension plan designed specifically for directors and key employees.
- It provides a comprehensive package of retirement benefits for such personnel, providing security in retirement and flexibility with valuable tax and investment advantages.
- Depending on length of service and final remuneration, the plan provides a pension of up to two thirds of final salary a year, if preferred increasable at maximum rate according to RPI, and is payable for life. (The maximum pension may be built up over a minimum of 20 years' service at the rate of 2/60 for each year.)
- Part of the pension can be commuted to a tax-free cash sum. The cash sum that can be taken is expressed as 3/80 of final remuneration for each year of service (up to a maximum of 40 years) or 2.25 times the planholder's pension, whichever is the greater, subject to a maximum of 1.5 times final salary. The maximum cash sum that may be taken is also dependent on at least 20 years' service to retirement.
- The security provided by this plan means that the prospect can become financially independent of his company, thereby enabling him to pass all his shares to his inheritors. He can thus mitigate inheritance tax upon his death.

POINTERS TO THE SALE OF CERTAIN PRODUCTS

- The prospect does not have to rely on his company profits for his retirement. He would be in a position to sell his shares only when the market is advantageous for him to do so.
- The company's contributions are allowable as a business expense and can be offset against liability for corporation tax. Although special rules apply to single contributions, they too can attract tax relief subject to careful planning.
- The prospect may also contribute up to 15 per cent of his salary to his executive retirement plan and obtain income tax relief at his highest rate. This 15 per cent of earnings is subject to a maximum earnings of £75,000 for 1992/93 (increasing in line with the Retail Prices Index). The pension investment fund is exempt from all income and capital gains taxes, thereby enabling the greatest possible growth of the fund. The retirement fund built up for the benefit of key employees is protected against future financial misfortune by being held in trust and does not therefore form part of the assets of the company.
- The plan can have provision for a spouse's pension and additional lump sum death benefit of up to four times salary in the event of death before retirement. These benefits can be paid directly to the prospect's beneficiaries without incurring any liability to inheritance tax.
- Upon the planholder's death after retirement, the maximum pension that can be provided for a widow(er) is two thirds of the maximum approvable planholder's pension. This is a very important benefit and must always be pointed out. Married prospects hardly ever fail to raise this particular issue.
- Contributions can be made monthly, annually or in single amounts. The contributions can be increased or decreased from renewal dates and this enables the company to make full use of tax concessions offered by the plan.
- The plan can be tailored to the individual circumstances of each person. Different contributions can be paid in respect of different key employees to provide varying levels (and types) of retirement benefits.
- The pension can be a fixed amount, or arranged to increase each year to protect against inflation. The

pension can also be guaranteed for a term of years (many plans are guaranteed for five or ten years). Therefore, should the plan member die the full pension continues to be paid, say to the spouse, for the term guaranteed.

Finally, by allowing you and your company (or the company that you, as an independent adviser, are recommending) to set up the executive pension plan, the prospect has the assurance that he is dealing with a leading company which has long experience in the field of looking after people's financial security, and which is backed by large assets.

It must be stressed again that this last point should be made only on condition that the description of you or the product company is strictly true otherwise it would not only be unethical but you would also be in breach of consumer protection legislation. This applies to whatever financial product or service you are selling (see Appendix).

Selling group schemes in general
The marketing of group schemes in general is potentially very lucrative, although subject to fierce competition.

Approaches can be made by telephone, preferably as a follow-up to an introductory letter, whether or not as a referred lead. Referrals from an existing client company will obviously carry special weight.

If your organisation, whether as broker or life assurance company, has a general insurance branch client bank in addition to its financial services client bank, then this will constitute a potentially very profitable source of leads, of which you should make full use. Apart from their obvious connection with your organisation, general insurance business leads are often qualified in your favour, because during the course of documentation for general insurance clients may have ticked a reply box indicating whether or not they are interested in financial services like life assurance or pensions.

These existing general insurance clients may have insured buildings, factories, business premises, cars or equipment, and are especially useful leads for the development of group schemes such as pensions (personal and executive), PHI, keyman insurance, etc. Your organisation has the goodwill, and

POINTERS TO THE SALE OF CERTAIN PRODUCTS

would be the natural choice to be given such business. This connection also gives you a useful advantage when attempting to get through to busy executives. You should write first to the responsible official, be it the proprietor, company secretary or managing director, and introduce yourself and your organisation, which will be known to him. State in your letter that you would like to ring him on a given day or week to inquire whether he would be prepared to have an initial discussion followed by written quotes upon the topic (such as group PHI) that you wish to bring to his attention. In order to forestall any initial request for literature when you ring him, it is a good idea to enclose some explanatory material on the subject, which you can expand upon and answer questions when you see him.

This approach is professional, it works and there is nothing about it that would antagonise a busy executive prospect. What is more, if the prospect is remotely interested he would *need* to see you, because in order to prepare quotes there is a fair amount that needs to be discussed, including details relating to the relevant staff members. Obviously for group business you will need to see this key executive prospect more than once.

When you first telephone and are put through to reception or a secretary, simply state your name and ask to speak to Mr Prospect. The odds are that you will be put through because you are now known and your call is expected. If asked to state the nature of your call (as in 'May I ask what it is in connection with?'), say that you are phoning about your letter. No harm is done if she rings through and comes back with the message that he thanks you for your letter but is not interested in your proposed scheme at present, or that his organisation has already taken care of this particular matter. Nothing ventured nothing gained!

When you are put through, you should be brief and to the point. 'Good morning Mr Prospect, thank you for taking my call. My name is John Smith of Sun Star. I am phoning in connection with my letter to you asking if I might be permitted to see you to discuss the possibility of group permanent health insurance (or, say, income replacement insurance) for members of your staff as explained in the brochure that I sent you. This would guarantee members of your staff a replacement income as long as necessary if they should fall ill. If you will allow me to see you I can take the relevant details in order to arrange quotes and also fill you in further. Would you care to make an appointment?' If he agrees to see you, arrange a date. 'I look forward to seeing you on Wednesday', and hang up. Avoid the temptation to sell over the phone. Your aim at this stage is to sell the appointment.

A word of caution: make sure that you eventually present to the person who has the final authority to take the decision, or that he or she is at least present. It is a good idea before you even write, to ring up and find out, without giving anything away, who is the person responsible for matters relating to the issue that you want to contact that person about. If during your telephone call or during your meeting you are informed that he will have to discuss it with his colleagues or board, then you should offer, indeed do your best to persuade, that you be allowed to meet and present to the appropriate person(s). When you do, identify and pay special attention to the key individual who is empowered to take the decision. If you are unsure who this is, it is possible to identify that person by noting from whom those present take their cue in sitting down, standing up or other manifestations of body language (see also Chapter 9 on communicating effectively and the Bibliography).

Before you find yourself in the presence of your prospect(s) make sure that you have all the relevant accessories such as any visual aids, business cards, literature and illustrative quotes. This is particularly important with executives and proprietors, who like to be sure that they are dealing with a competent professional. Conscientious after-sales service will also pay special dividends here in the form of smooth running and probable lucrative future business.

Permanent health insurance
Permanent health insurance policies are among the easiest of plans to sell. This is because they have hitherto been undersold and also because loss of income arising from ill health, sickness or injury presents an immediate threat in the prospect's mind.

Buying life assurance is often motivated by prudence and concern for one's dependants, whereas buying permanent health insurance involves an additional concern for one's own position and prospects in the event of loss or diminution of income. Consequently it is easier to sell.

POINTERS TO THE SALE OF CERTAIN PRODUCTS

In my experience there are three effective approaches to its sale. The first is to raise the issue directly when on the phone to your prospect. The second is to undertake a marketing exercise by post specifically describing the product and its benefits and inviting the prospect to reply in a pre-paid envelope. Thirdly, and most commonly, during my interview with a prospect to discuss his financial planning I find a suitable opportunity to say, 'There is one other important matter I wish to raise with you. Do you have income protection in the event of illness or accident? This is a form of assurance whereby if you are unable to work due to ill health or accident, then after an initial deferment period of your choice you will be paid an income of up to 75 per cent of your previous annual earnings for as long as it takes, even up to your potential retirement age if you were never to be able to work again.'

Note that the first straightforward question is designed to draw his attention to the topic and where he has not heard of it before, to arouse his simple curiosity. Then comes the description which is brief but accurate and clearly and simply emphasises the benefits. The two components of gaining attention and describing benefits in two relatively brief sentences makes for maximum receptivity on the part of the prospect. I then ask how long he would be on full salary (or have an income if self-employed) in the event of such an unfortunate occurrence, and we agree on a suitable deferment period after it is pointed out that the longer the deferment period obviously the lower the premiums would be. I then suggest that he allows me to give him an idea of the cost and reach into my briefcase for my rate book. Unless he already has PHI, a prospect will invariably at least indicate interest. I then calculate the cost based on benefit of about 75 per cent of current weekly income and fall silent to allow him to reflect, and await his response. It is important to be succinct and not verbose in order to give him a chance to consider it without interruption and possibly ask some questions.

If the prospect does not already have any permanent health insurance there is at least a 50 per cent, if not odds on, chance that he will give you the go-ahead there and then. If he insists that he wants to think about it, do remember to ask if there is

SELLING LIFE ASSURANCE AND FINANCIAL PRODUCTS

anything that you can further clarify for him. You may still be able to close, but if not maintain continuity by offering to arrange a written quotation to be sent to him. Leave some literature and arrange to ring back after he has received the quotes. He will more than likely agree to this.

Sales of permanent health insurance should greatly expand in the future as it is increasingly brought to the attention of the working public. You too should therefore take advantage of this trend.

Savings and investments plans
These include products such as qualifying with profits and unit-linked type endowment policies, non-qualifying unit-linked savings plans, unit trusts, personal equity plans and other lump sum investments. Remember to emphasise any tax concessions attached to these plans such as the fact that the proceeds of a qualifying policy are free of income and capital gains tax upon maturity, death or encashment after ten years (or three quarters of the term if less) – otherwise, if encashed before the required minimum term, there could be some higher rate (but not basic rate) tax payable, or any age allowance to which the prospect is entitled could be affected.

Your first task is to identify a need for such a plan from your initial factfinding exercise, unless the prospect himself indicates that he needs one. For example, he may be the parent of a newly born child and wants to plan in time for school fees. This purpose can be met, as you are no doubt aware by a series of endowment savings plans maturing in the years that the fees will be required, or a flexible savings plan split up into different policies where the individual segments can be made to mature in the years that the fees are required, without commitment to a fixed term from the outset.

Once you have identified a need you should then draw attention to it and explain the features, clearly pointing out the benefits of the product and how it will serve its purpose of meeting that need. This should serve to make the prospect aware of the product's suitability and therefore desire it, provided there are no remaining doubts in his mind about any aspect of the product. You must look out for any such doubts and clarify and reassure as and when necessary.

POINTERS TO THE SALE OF CERTAIN PRODUCTS

Don't just wade in there without any thought for the client's position, hell-bent on making a sale, and start rabbiting on about the plan that will give you the highest commission. This is both unethical as well as counterproductive in the long run. Your task is to establish yourself in his mind as his valued adviser in financial matters pertaining to your field, and be seen to take the trouble to establish what is in his best interests.

When explaining the purpose of a plan, an effective way of illustrating its special benefits and suitability for that purpose is to compare it with the features and benefits of a valid but alternative type of well-known scheme that falls somewhat short of fully meeting the prospect's need and required purpose.

Let us take an example. A schoolmaster who has sufficient life assurance in addition to making free-standing additional voluntary contributions to his pension scheme is saving all his spare income, amounting to £150 per month, with a building society. He has a young child he may wish to educate privately. You recommend a flexible unit-linked savings plan with an insurance company that has a good track record.

First point out that there are differing approaches to efficient savings, depending upon whether one intends to save short term or over the medium to long term, the two being mutually complementary. Point out that he should save short term (say up to five years) with a building society for money that he may require at short notice for whatever reason. This is practical and desirable for the purpose. It won't make him a fortune but the money is earning as much in interest as it reasonably can. It should stay there safely in case it is needed.

However, it is the amount per month he can comfortably syphon off over the longer term that should go into a savings plan, but point out that if he takes out such a plan and then drops it within three to four years there cannot be any certainty of gain and he may indeed lose. Over the minimum length of time that such investment plans are designed to run, however, no building society savings scheme would be able to match the overall return of even a reasonably performing endowment or unit-linked savings plan, paid out free of capital gains and income tax. You can point out that interest rates would have to remain exceptionally high for an unrealistically long period to do so. Furthermore, point out that although there are no guarantees in this business, the expectation is of a healthy capital growth of the underlying fund and consequent payout with a company that has a good investment or bonus track record, which is why he is expected to take a theoretically minor risk for the sake of a higher gain. No thinking person would object to this. By pointing out and comparing the suitability for different aims of the two types of savings, you have successfully illustrated that the product you are recommending will best serve his need and purpose. You can convey the potentially effective message that you have given thought to his position and add weight to your case by a statement like, 'This is the best recommendation that I can make for this purpose'. Provided that you match the correct plan to the prospect's correct need you should have a high degree of success in selling investment plans. The opportunities are there.

Mortgages
Offering to place mortgages on behalf of prospects is a useful way of eliciting responses from them, for example with a mailshot. The appeal of helping people to buy their own home is a powerful one. However, I would not rely solely on mailshots to sell financial products such as mortgage endowment policies, pension plans or other products that can be linked to mortgage repayment schemes. This method of prospecting should only complement other methods. A lot can go wrong. You could place a mortgage only to have the client pull out for reasons ranging from getting a better interest rate elsewhere to losing the property.

A further word of caution. Do not under any circumstances complete the sale of a policy on the promise that you will obtain a mortgage for that client at some indeterminate date in the near or distant future. This is not entirely honest and can lead you into difficulties later if you fail to come up with the goods at the required time.

I recommend that you always arrange to open a building society account for all clients that you see if they don't already have one – and if they do, open a second one. You can do this through a couple of building societies with whom you can establish friendly informal connections and build up good will by introducing funds. You may even be able to obtain a

POINTERS TO THE SALE OF CERTAIN PRODUCTS

mortgage allocation: this would be particularly useful when mortgage funds are tight. Tell your clients when you see them about other matters to approach their own building society first when seeking a mortgage, followed by other local societies if necessary. You can offer to step in and help if they fail or are not happy with any mortgage offers they have secured, or if they fail to secure one altogether. Advance planning will make it easier for you and your client later on.

When you are approached for help in attempting to obtain a mortgage, I suggest that you first take down all relevant details without making a promise, and offer to ring the prospective client back within a given time. A lending institution may or may not agree to consider an application based on the details that you have passed on. You should make it clear on what terms, such as the interest rate, a prospective lender is willing to consider an application. Do not fudge or raise false hopes for the sake of making a sale. At the same time don't allow yourself to be messed about by the prospect. Either he decides to go ahead and apply or he does not.

If the prospect agrees to submit a mortgage application you should complete the application form and simultaneously submit a proposal form for the chosen policy on behalf of the client. You should do this after having discussed and advised him on the most suitable type of policy to pay off such a mortgage. Make sure that you explain all the options open to him. For example, it may well be that he would prefer a pension mortgage if eligible, rather than an endowment one.

Once the mortgage application and the proposal form for the endowment policy have been submitted, you should instruct the life assurance company to consider the application and issue an acceptance. However, unless the client specifies otherwise, you should instruct the company that the proposed policy is not to go on risk and that premiums are not to be collected preferably at least until the formal mortgage offer is made and contracts on the property are about to be exchanged. Some clients even prefer to leave it until the date of completion, although this may be cutting it fine because the lender will soon be pressing for the policy. You should arrange for the client to inform you when the formal offer is about to take place and at the same time to let you have his instructions to arrange for the policy to go on risk. The policy document should be ready preferably immediately after the completion date, and passed on to the lender with a copy for the client/policy holder. You can arrange for the insurance company to send the policy document directly to the lender, or you can deliver it yourself to the borrower and policyholder, who will pass it on to the lender who then holds it as security. You may also be asked by the client to send the policy to his solicitor to pass on to the building society or other lender.

When you first submit the proposal form for a policy, I suggest that you simultaneously write to the prospective lender (or request the life assurance company to do so) giving precise details of the proposed policy. This information is very useful to the building society or other lender even though brief details would already be available on the lender's mortgage application form. They will then know that the policy due to turn up is correct and suitable for the mortgage in all essential respects. They also have the opportunity to raise any queries before the policy goes on risk.

When you first see a prospective client about a mortgage case, he may well understandably not wish to take up the policy until the last possible moment. You can accommodate this feeling and still do business as described above because there is a procedure that must be adhered to and a deadline before which a policy must be in existence. The client has nothing to lose and everything to gain by submitting a proposal form for consideration prior to its taking effect. Do point out that getting this particular piece of paperwork out of the way leaves him free to concentrate on the other necessary aspects of his property purchase. If the transaction falls through, the policy does not take effect and he does not have to pay any premiums. Do bear in mind and point out that even if any adjustment becomes necessary – such as to the sum to be assured – this can be accommodated and dealt with by the insurance company before the risk date.

You will find that most clients see the sense in these arrangements and agree to set the process in motion.

7
The Skills of Persuasion

Even after you have identified a prospective client's needs, the fact still remains that to sell any, especially complex, financial product which requires a large immediate or long-term financial commitment can require persuasion and its associated skills.

A substantial part of these skills has to do with the psychology of persuasion. It is the deployment of these skills that distinguishes the very best salespeople of consistently high performance from the merely competent. These skills can be mastered; they are used consciously or instinctively by all the best persuaders in whatever field involving an audience.

The techniques involved are allied to those used in clinical hypnosis. In any successful persuasion, the aim is initially to create a state of heightened attention and receptivity in the subject or audience, leading to a better disposition to what you have to say. Let me hasten to add here that there is no suggestion that the subject is led into any form of trance or deprived of the ability to think for himself.

The best persuaders build trust by reflecting the thoughts, tone of voice, rhythm and rate of speech and the mood of their prospect(s) or other listening audience (again, the techniques of the clinical hypnotist). A usually fast and loud speaking salesman may find himself talking back in a soft, slow rhythmic voice to a slow speaking prospective client, matching his rhythm of speech and opening the meeting with a series of mild and factual statements about the weather and continuing cold and rain. What he is doing is encouraging the prospect into a mood of trust, empathy and rapport by identifying with, and matching, his verbal and emotional make-up.

The somewhat provocative confirmation that a successful sales presentation involves an intuitive form of indirect hypnosis was arrived at by an American psychologist, Donald

SELLING LIFE ASSURANCE AND FINANCIAL PRODUCTS

A. Moine, in a study that he performed in 1981. His initial study involved eight life assurance salesmen, four of whom were classed as top producers by their companies and four as only average. The two groups were then closely matched on such factors as age and experience. Taking the role of prospective client he spoke with the eight men, recording their comments and analysing them for the thirty techniques of persuasion that two others, Richard Bandler and John Grinder, had previously identified in the work of a master hypnotist, Milton Erikson. He also examined the sales techniques of fourteen top sellers from other fields such as real estate, luxury cars, stocks (i.e. equities) and commodities. He then tested his findings with more than fifty people who sold, amongst other things, jets, computers, oil and gas leases. His conclusion, which many successful persuaders reflecting upon their own skills may also have reached, was that experienced and better skilled salespeople essentially use the techniques of the clinical hypnotist whereas mediocre ones do not.

The relevant techniques can be classified into rules that you can learn and put to use. The whole idea is the perfectly legitimate aim of relaxing your prospect and gaining his attention and goodwill so that he is receptive to what you have to say without becoming defensive, negative or sceptical without good cause – one would certainly not be depriving a prospect of his critical faculties.

The principal techniques involved are set out below.

Synchronising With One's Audience

One should first establish a mood of empathy, trust and rapport by means of 'hypnotic pacing'. This involves statements and gestures that reflect a prospect's behaviour, feelings and reactions. This is what the best salespeople do. Pacing is an outward reflection and matching of the prospect's current mental and emotional mood suggesting 'We are similar! I am thinking and feeling as you do. We are on the same wavelength. You can trust me.'

The simplest form of pacing is best described as 'descriptive pacing', in which the seller pronounces accurate, if neutral, descriptions of the prospect's experience. 'It's been awfully cold these last few days, hasn't it?' 'You said you were going to take your exams for promotion in October. I hope they went well.' These statements, especially at the beginning of one's meeting, serve the purpose of establishing agreement and developing affinity, between you the salesperson and the prospective client. In a comparative statement a hypnotist might say, 'You are here today to let me help you with a problem which you have told me about.' Salespeople who are only average or inexperienced tend to launch straight into a memorised, rigid sales pitch or immediately start to bombard the prospect with a barrage of questions before first attempting to break the ice and create empathy. If one neglects to pace the prospect then one creates no common ground on which to build confidence and trust.

In another type of pacing described as 'objective pacing' the prospect objects, or in some other way resists, and you agree and match your response to those of the prospect. A skilled life assurance salesperson might agree that a *certain* life assurance policy is not exactly the best type of investment just as a clinical hypnotist might tell a resistant subject, 'You are resisting going into a trance. Don't worry. That's perfectly all right.' Thus the salesperson, having agreed with the prospect's objection, then leads the prospect to a position that neutralises the objection. The salesperson who agrees that a certain type of life assurance policy is not the best type of investment perhaps goes on to tell the prospect, 'but it does have its uses that apply specifically to yourself.' He then describes all the benefits of that particular life assurance policy. The mistake of a lesser salesperson would be to respond to the objection head on with arguments that attempt to counter the prospect's objection. This, in turn, will often lead the prospect to stand his ground more stubbornly.

Pacing can also be used very effectively by how something is said rather than by what is said. The good salesman has, or develops, the ability to pace the language and thought pattern of any prospective client. There is a hypnotic effect when the skilled salesperson matches the tone of voice, rhythm, volume and rate of speech of the prospect. He also mirrors the prospect's body language and mood. If the prospect crosses his legs the skilled salesman will also tend to cross his legs. If the prospect leans forward he too tends to lean slightly forward. If the prospect smiles or frowns his expression mirrors that of the prospect.

The skilled salesperson even adopts the distinctive verbal characteristics of the prospect's language, copying phrases such as 'makes sense', 'rings a bell', the eventual pay-out', 'if we go for that'. If the prospect is feeling slightly tired or depressed the salesperson sympathises and shares that feeling admitting that he too has been feeling a bit low lately. One is essentially sharing and reflecting the prospective client's perceptions and sense of reality.

There is, however, one area where a skilled salesperson should not necessarily reflect or pace a prospective client's behaviour and attitudes and this is in the area of personal beliefs and values. I remember one occasion when I went to see a prospective client who bluntly told me less than half way into the presentation that he was now a Marxist and did not believe in such exploitative, capitalist solutions. I certainly did not share his beliefs and I was not going to pretend that I did. I fell momentarily silent, smiled, and with what I hoped he would take as being said in good humour, I replied, 'Well, this is the best thing available for your future financial security until the revolution comes.' I thus hoped to make clear to him that we would agree to differ on this, at the risk of sounding sarcastic.

Where you encounter a less rigid stance it is useful to display polite interest and any knowledge that you may have of the beliefs to which your prospect subscribes. You may even choose to discuss them briefly and make clear your respect for his opinions, even if you do not happen to share them. If anything, a display of interest in other peoples' beliefs helps to break down barriers and create affinity and rapport. One then gently but firmly passes back to the main subject for discussion. I have had some very pleasant conversations with clients from varying walks of life holding a variety of views upon many topics. Some become good and valued friends.

When a salesperson shares a prospect's strongly held views, he should be careful of agreeing too forcefully in order to avoid giving the prospect the impression that 'talk is cheap; it doesn't cost him anything to agree or say what he says'.

Soft Selling
It is only after a skilled salesperson has created the necessary environment of rapport and put himself properly in the picture regarding a prospect's circumstances, that he begins to introduce the suggestions which he hopes will induce the prospect to buy. One such soft technique is to use obviously accurate pronouncements as links to introduce influencing statements that lead to the desired response or action. For example: 'You are thirty-five years old; you are presently the sole breadwinner maintaining a family of wife and two children on a very adequate income of £25,000 a year. We recommend that you need life assurance of £175,000'. These pacing and leading statements are akin to the way a hypnotist leads a client into hypnosis: 'You are sitting comfortably, you are relaxed and you are listening to my voice.' Note the unarguable pacing statements, and 'Your eyelids are getting heavier and beginning to close'.

There is in fact no need for there to be any logical connection between the pacing statement and the leading statement as illustrated above. They can be completely unrelated, yet when the two are connected they exert a powerful persuasive logic that can be effective even with such usually analytical and rational prospects as lawyers, doctors or academics. The power of the leading statement arises from the fact that it capitalises on the positive mental state built by the unquestionably true pacing statement. In my opinion, however, one must always have ready the strictly factual or logical reason for one's suggestion or leading statement if challenged. In our example the prospect may well suddenly ask, 'Why £175,000?' To which one gives the hopefully sensible reply, 'If you take away the life assurance covering your mortgage, which is to pay off the mortgage if need be, you need cover of at least seven times your current salary if the income from the proceeds is to come even near to maintaining your family at their current standard of living.'

Once the logical reason for your original suggestion is appreciated, its effect should be to reinforce it. In fact, in my experience, the persuasive effect of the suggestion or leading statement can often be further reinforced by voluntarily following it up with the reasons for the suggestion. For example, you may have suggested to a client that he should take out a unit-linked savings plan; you can follow it up with the perfectly valid reason that his savings from current income should not all go into a building society. It should be split between an interest-bearing shortish-term savings account with a building society, where he can get his hands on the cash in an emergency with another portion committed over a five-year term with a TESSA account for the sake of tax-free interest, while the amount that he can comfortably syphon off and forget about for, say, at least ten years should go into a qualifying and good with-profits or well managed unit-linked investment policy for the sake of a potentially much better return free of income and capital gains tax. If the reasoning cannot be flawed then the persuasive effect of the initial suggestion, or influencing/leading statement becomes that much more powerful, given the now well disposed and receptive mind of the prospect.

A prospect who has agreed with what a salesman has so far said expects instinctively to agree with him further, just as a prospect who has disagreed looks out for and expects something further to disagree with. It is important therefore not to disrupt the positive atmosphere and flow of the discussion by saying something that may throw a spanner in the works.

A skilled salesperson can ensure receptivity by the prospect to 'embedded commands' in the form of sensible professional advice, by delivering his message with properly varying tone (pitch and inflection), rhythm and volume of speech. An embedded command is the message of what step he ought to take cloaked within an acceptable or true statement. As he pronounces his so-called 'command' he will slow down his speech, look the prospect in the eye and say each word slowly and deliberately: 'You will find that this is one of the most effective and tax-efficient methods of investment in the UK at this time' (an eminently suitable description of a personal equity plan). A favourite of mine is 'If you ask yourself what is the best way that I can save £80 a month from current income over a period of ten years plus, you will find that this is one of the two most advantageous methods available in the UK today' – with the other method preferably also among the range of schemes that you can sell.

THE SKILLS OF PERSUASION

Stories, Metaphors and Anecdotes

Finally, an important tool in a good salesperson's armoury is the use of relevant stories, anecdotes and the framing of comments in metaphors to enable a prospect to see things his way. Top salespeople routinely use them to influence prospective clients.

Stories can be effective in securing client attention and building rapport, while at the same time illustrating or impressing upon a prospect the features, benefits and unique selling points of a product. They can also be used to emphasise and drive home a valid point: 'I fixed up a unit-linked, whole-of-life policy for a thirty-five-year-old business man yesterday. What appealed to him was the flexibility whereby he could reduce the high life assurance involved to its bare minimum when the children have grown up and he no longer felt the high cover was necessary. That way he can then divert most of the premiums to investment to build up the value of the policy.'

Metaphors and stories can be used to handle objections and subsequently close without endangering goodwill and rapport. On one occasion I was attempting to sell the low-cost mortgage endowment policy of a highly reputable life assurance society, one of my favourites, to a somewhat price-conscious client. I went to see him equipped with quotations from the organisation in the knowledge that I was recommending quality. On meeting him I noticed that he had another set of quotations on the table provided by another source whose rates seemed to be somewhat lower but whose past record of investment returns was not nearly as good. After some discussions of both, I thought I'd make my position clear, 'I want to emphasise,' I said, 'that the principal reason for taking out a low-cost mortgage endowment policy is to pay off the mortgage at the end of the day, *and* hopefully leave yourself with as much of a surplus as the bonuses will manage to produce. This organisation's reputation and bonus record, as you are no doubt aware, are second to none. It's a bit like taking your family on a long air journey. You have the choice of either going on a reliable, but inferior, aircraft more cheaply, or the most up-to-date aircraft run by a leading airline. Which would you have more peace of mind with, even though they would both get you there?'

The purpose here is not to rubbish the other company. This could prove counter-productive, apart from being inaccurate and unfair. The purpose is to focus his attention directly onto his principal concern. In this analogy it is his family's greatest possible safety and comfort rather than the comparative cost of the air passage. The clear implication regarding the matter at hand was that he had two choices that were clearly unequal. The policy that I was recommending would give him a more worry-free ride to his eventual mortgage pay-off and the potentially highest possible cash surplus (judging from the organisation's reputation and past performance). The metaphor emphasised the principal consideration that clearly outweighed the alternative. Being fairly knowledgeable in these matters he nodded saying, 'Yes, I take your point. We'll go for company X.' He has not regretted his decision.

Another point to note in this example is that the issue to which the reservation related (i.e. price) is expanded in order to encompass and then emphasise a more crucial topic of greater potential concern to the prospect than mere cost. As an Italian friend of mine, who runs a successful restaurant chain, once said, 'If they say the prices are high, I reply, "But the food is better!".'

Anecdotes, stories or metaphors should be brief and not verbose so that you hold the prospect's attention span, and also to give the point that you wish to emphasise the greatest possible impact. How you say it is as important as what you say. The often intuitively hypnotic techniques outlined in this chapter are, of course, not just confined to good salesmen. They are also used by the best public speakers, politicians, barristers and preachers. They are even used by counsellors and social workers who have to relax, create empathy with, and talk to sometimes tense, anxious and even difficult people. They are also persuaders who, just as much as salespeople, try to influence their audiences and attempt to instil into them a resolve to do something or to secure agreement to their viewpoint.

If, in addition to the techniques and rules of good selling outlined in the earlier chapters, you utilise the skills described in this chapter, you should significantly increase your selling effectiveness, especially in terms of sales per number of prospects seen.

8
Client Profiles and Differences in Client Temperament

It is essential that you take into account differences in personality and temperament, as well as intelligence and relevant technical knowledge, among the different prospects that you meet. They will after all represent a cross section of society, and you need to be alert to these differences and to respond to them in the manner most likely to establish mutual cooperation and obtain results. Here we deal with some of the more usual general types.

The Self-Confident Client
Provided that you are technically knowledgeable and conduct your factfind and presentation properly, you will find that the more self-confident and intelligent a prospective client the more of a pleasure it is to present to him and consequently easier to sell to. Since your presentation is easily understood by the prospect and his queries are usually pertinent to the issue under discussion, the product sells itself as he readily appreciates its relevance to his position. All outstanding matters tend to be easily resolved and dealt with to his satisfaction: for example, you may be questioned about details that a less alert or less knowledgeable client may ignore or fail to pick upon, like the management charges attaching to investment funds or a comparison of such charges between various different funds.

Such clients may also ask for a comparison of the relative merits of alternative products they have heard or read about that can serve a similar purpose. They may then ask you for your recommendation. You must be up to date and knowledgeable with such advice. Your reasons need to bear weight if you are to convince such a prospect and have your judgement respected. If you are unable to provide him with the necessary information, be honest about it and offer to obtain it or do the required research and get back to him. This is always appreciated and tends to raise you in his estimation, assuming of course that the matter is not something that you should have been able to resolve on the spot. The more professional that you are seen to be the better your chances of concluding a sale.

The percentage of repeat future business with this type of client is very high due both to the client's own intelligence and self-confidence, and to the professional respect and confidence that you have earned. He knows his own mind and is therefore usually decisive. This means that you can conclude business at the earliest suitable moment without any dithering on his part.

The Pedantic Client

There is the kind of client who tends to be pedantic and needs to go into more than usual detail, dotting all the I's and crossing all the T's of a product, its features, its benefits and its purpose before he is happy about it. This happens even though he may or may not have any background knowledge.

You need to be patient and it may be a little frustrating with this sort of person but it can be ultimately rewarding – provided you help him make up his mind. You must be as accurate, clear and precise as possible. Speak slowly; you should often repeat what you say more than once because repetition, say of a fact, together with unambiguous clarity and precision has a reassuring effect with this kind of client. Do not leave room for any doubt about the meaning of what you say. You must not give the impression that you are avoiding a question or skirting round an issue. Make sure that you can logically and factually justify any claims that you make to avoid being challenged about them later. If, however, he raises some totally irrelevant objection or issue, try to give him a satisfactory and accurate reply while at the same time tactfully pointing out that he is slightly off course.

Usually such prospects, when they have little or no knowledge of financial planning, do look to you for advice and reassurance. So long as you respond to them in the correct manner and they comprehend and appreciate what you say, they will

CLIENT PROFILES AND DIFFERENCES IN CLIENT TEMPERAMENT

be reassured and happy enough in their own mind to agree to take up the recommendations that you make. What is more they will be especially appreciative of the patience you displayed, and you will be the first person they contact when they next need advice.

The Arrogant Client

There is another type of prospect who can appear abrupt, arrogant and conceited. (If you judge this to be due to shyness it is important to put him at ease.) He often lacks any knowledge of financial planning but does not like to admit it. He may try to put you on the defensive and he is also the type most likely to keep you waiting or even to stand you up on your appointment. Often this is a power-play tactic intended to establish dominance. If he keeps you waiting long after the appointed time – say, twenty minutes to half-an-hour – enquire from reception or his secretary what the delay is and offer to reschedule the appointment since you are running to a schedule. Make it clear that you too are a busy person. If you cannot be reassured and see him soon after, or reschedule the appointment, then leave your card, say you'll ring back and leave.

During discussion a client of this type may come up with such gems of information as 'I know; I am not stupid' (perish the thought!). Such types do tend to be a little snobbish but hard working, ambitious and do genuinely want the best possible financial product and arrangement for whatever purpose they have in mind. They often tend not to be too trusting and may well have read up in the financial press on any subject they intend to discuss prior to your visit. You had better be up to date and know what you are talking about.

You need to make every effort to win the 'arrogant' client's trust and confidence in you in every manner possible. Stay cool and confident. Do not allow yourself to be rattled by any snide comment like 'I know you want to flog me this policy' or by any question that you may find difficulty in replying to there and then. Put the onus on him to put you as much as possible in the picture about himself and his circumstances, and let him tell you what he would like you to do for him. Compliment him on his financial acumen and for being 'on the ball'. Agree with him where possible as confirmation of his good judgement. Spell out your recommendations and their reasons. React with confidence and precision to any objections or flaws he attempts to find. Where possible arouse curiosity with your superior knowledge of your own field. This will often ensure respectful attention, especially if he is prone to interrupt.

Be firm but friendly and courteous, and don't raise your voice. Pay special attention to the advice given in Chapter 7 on persuasion. Make it obvious to him that it is you who are the expert in your field, and stand your ground regarding your well thought-out opinions and suggestions. Don't apologise unnecessarily just for the sake of it unless he has a legitimate complaint, for example, relating to past dealings with your organisation. The more confident you appear, the more receptive and respectful you will notice he becomes. You need to allay his insecurities, but avoid obvious flattery as this can be counterproductive. If he is stubborn, with rigid ideas, appear to be sympathetic and understanding towards his viewpoint.

Again, this type of prospect will not buy unless he clearly understands the principal features and benefits, thus relating the product to his needs and causing him to want it. As I have previously pointed out you need to draw out any doubts and deal with them. This basically is an interested type of client but not always too secure. He needs to be satisfied and reassured on all matters that seem relevant to him before he will decide to buy.

The Smart Alec

You will encounter some prospects, thankfully not many, who make up for their lack of knowledge or intelligence, or both, by being too clever by half and pretending to know it all.

Avoid a confrontational approach and make sure that you do not directly contradict him or get into an argument. Listen to what he says. Use tact and compliments such as 'You seem well informed'. Hold his attention and arouse his curiosity by imparting information and facts that (a) he doesn't know and (b) are directly relevant to his interests. Politely stand your ground on matters that you know best and don't appear over-

CLIENT PROFILES AND DIFFERENCES IN CLIENT TEMPERAMENT

eager to sell. Flatter his ego, especially during the closing stages of a presentation by suggesting 'as you will no doubt be aware'.

Don't allow him to waste your time either. Having made your view clear, place the ball in his court and ask him bluntly whether he agrees with your recommendation or not. You will often discover that he will readily get off his high horse and defer to your better judgement. If he doesn't then there is no need to stay a moment longer than necessary. Leave your card and ask him to call you when he decides.

The Stubborn and Illogical Client

You may also occasionally find yourself in front of a prospect who is simply deaf to all logic, raises totally irrelevant and unjustifiable objections or belittles the product or service that you are recommending. He often has entrenched ideas and opinions.

Do not allow yourself to get drawn into an argument. A good approach is to appeal to his emotions without going over the top. For example, the life policy in question will pay out so much in the event of his death, sufficient to keep his family at a certain level of income. Its purpose is plain. Does he want peace of mind (emotion) or not? He has a clear choice. As long as you have made clear to him the benefits of a product, tell him bluntly that this is the best you can offer and that you are happy to abide by his decision. Once you have made it clear that he can take it or leave it, you will usually find that his decision is a favourable one.

The Charmer

There is also the type of prospect who will greet you for the first time in a charming friendly manner, nod eagerly and agree with all that you say and recommend, but when it comes to the crunch will simply refuse to be tied down to a decision.

You should ensure that your factfinding questions openly expose his needs and that he is therefore obliged expressly to acknowledge them. When he answers a factfind question which glaringly exposes any need, pause a moment longer than you would normally, and say something like 'We'll make a special note of that' before you carry on to the next question. Also ask him questions to which the replies will commit him to seek a solution to his problem(s): 'To what extent are you keen to provide for yourself the highest possible income in retirement?' Any intelligent reply to such a question would indicate that he would be very keen.

The above categories are, by necessity, generalised profiles of some types of clients that I have come across and which you are also bound to meet, or have already met. There are, of course, other types and one comes to recognise them with time. By treating them in a manner suited to their temperament you should increase your chances of producing a meeting of minds.

It is always important to bear in mind that a proper factfinding exercise and adherence to the rules of correct presentation – which include the correct handling of queries and objections – apply to all cases. It is principally upon these that you stand or fall when attempting to make a sale.

9
How to Communicate Effectively

The methods for the successful selling of financial products set out so far in this book can be enhanced to good effect by using the principles of effective communication. The rules involved are applicable generally to most forms of communication, not just to selling. They can involve business meetings, political discussions or social conversation; they are, however, especially relevant to selling. Quite simply, if you are a poor communicator you will not be the most effective and successful of financial product salespersons. We can classify communication skills as verbal (including written) and non-verbal communication.

We are mostly concerned here with verbal communication. We have all heard people on radio and television or in private conversation who, while perfectly qualified to express a viewpoint or comment upon a topic of interest, go on and on, fail to hold our attention or rapidly lose it, or cannot express themselves succinctly and clearly. It may be a member of the public, or a member of a certain profession invited to speak and enlighten us. Compare such performances with the concise and structured clarity with which a skilled communicator such as a minister of the Crown conveys his or her point. Whether you agree or disagree, you hang on to every word and sentence and follow the reasoning of what is being said. Your emotions are aroused for or against, but at least they have been successfully aroused to fury or to support. Names that come to mind are Tony Benn and Enoch Powell on opposite sides of the political spectrum; others are Dr David Owen and Dennis Healy. In the past, men like Churchill and Lloyd George held people spellbound. A non-political example is Dr Jonathan Miller, the physician and opera director. When such people speak, every word and sentence strikes home to convey a picture in our mind and imagination. The compact timescale within which they make their point makes for maximum impact and comprehension.

The time constraints imposed on speakers by radio and television are in fact a blessing because, as we shall see, brevity is crucial to getting one's point across successfully. Most of us have come across verbose salespeople that one wants to avoid at all costs. In fact, the stereotype characteristics of a salesperson that people shirk from most is verbosity and pressure selling. In the minds of most people these go together.

No person whose job it is to sell, especially something as abstract as financial products, can be described as competent until he or she becomes an effective communicator. The same communication skills that make one a better salesperson will also enable that person to communicate effectively in all other areas of life where human communication is called for, be it selling, teaching, telling a good story, debating or public speaking.

The principles outlined below will enable you to gain a listener's attention, hold his interest and convey your point effectively so that he comprehends and appreciates what you say. We can't all be good-looking, but we can all make ourselves welcome company, and being an effective communicator is one of the ways of doing this.

Brevity
Have you ever switched into a local commercial radio phone-in programme and found yourself listening to some long-winded bore going on and on about an otherwise interesting topic without getting to the point? The programme presenter acknowledges his contribution and cuts him off as quickly as is decently possible, often with a curt remark, hoping that Fred in Tooting might have something brief to say. The outstanding presenter of this type of programme was the late George Gale on LBC in the seventies, who with his orderly, razor-sharp mind and wonderfully gravelly voice could, in a few short words, highlight and analyse the core of any issue, as well as put down woolly-minded callers.

The essential prerequisite to effective communication is brevity in making your point. Keep it short and sweet. Any point or message that you want to get across should be delivered within about half a minute. That is the attention span of an individual for assimilating a given point. It is more effective to make your individual point in about thirty seconds than to convey it in two, five or fifteen minutes. Whether you have more time or not you need to grab your listener's attention, convey the heart of the matter, and obtain the desired effect of convincing or explaining within that half minute.

This doesn't mean that you need to talk fast. It does mean that you have to choose your words carefully and avoid unnecessary verbiage. Any extra time you may have should be preliminary preparation or elaboration of a point already made. The reason for this is that no matter how long you talk for (or for that matter how much you write) and no matter how much time a listener can spare, the attention span of the average person to absorb and process a message is in fact half a minute. That is why most radio and television commercials are of thirty seconds' duration. Similarly, if you concentrate on an inanimate object your mind will begin to wander after about thirty seconds. This is not to say that the discourse itself cannot last longer. Once the thirty-second message has been conveyed and absorbed, it is possible to recapture attention by introducing an allied or different message. Similarly, if the inanimate object referred to above was a lamp and it moved, or switched off and on, or changed colour, it would recapture your attention for another thirty seconds. This is why every time you read a new paragraph your attention span starts afresh.

Once you consciously think in terms of efficient communication, you will develop clarity of thought when speaking (and writing). You will be logical and your delivery will become clear and concise. Your contribution in conversation will become effective whether you are presenting or questioning.

Clarity of purpose
There is no point in even opening your mouth or putting pen to paper unless you know clearly what it is you want to achieve. What exactly is the point you wish to make? Why are you having a given conversation? Uncertainty about your objective results in woolly thinking, uncertainty as to self expression and choice of words. You end up achieving nothing by what you say.

SELLING LIFE ASSURANCE AND FINANCIAL PRODUCTS

Our principal concern in this book is selling financial products. Wanting to sell a given product to a prospective client is a good example of a clear objective or purpose. You have identified a client's needs and have located the correct matching product. This is a legitimate ancillary objective in itself. Now your objective switches to the task of selling the product by highlighting the features and convincing the prospect of the benefits; that it will satisfy his needs and meet his purpose. You thus create the desire to buy, because the prospect is convinced that this is the product he wants. So you see, within an overall objective or aim there can be clear *sub*-objectives that you need to reach before reaching your main objective.

The same applies whether you see your manager to ask for increased commission or whether you contact a firm to complain, and ask for your money back. It is the same in all cases. *For any communication to be effective you must have a clear aim.* Otherwise don't bother.

Identify your correct listener target
It is not much use getting an appointment and making out a convincing case to someone for buying a product, or undertaking any course of action, if your listener does not have the full authority to act in the way you would like him to. I have already referred to this in the section on selling group schemes. As I pointed out, you simply *must* make out your case to the party or parties ultimately responsible for taking a decision. Similarly, it is absolutely essential that you bring a spouse or partner into any discussion if he or she has at least an equal say in taking a decision or needs to be consulted. If you are faced with a situation where that key person is absent, you should try to arrange another presentation in the presence of such a key person. The same is true for other situations. If you have a complaint regarding something sold to you or for services rendered and you demand satisfaction or your money back, there is no point taking it up with somebody who doesn't have the authority to rectify the situation. If you demand satisfaction you need to target the person who can give you satisfaction – nobody else will do.

Having identified the correct target individual, however, you need, as far as possible, to *assess* that person, to place yourself in his position and ask yourself 'What does that person expect of me?', 'What would I want if I was him or her?'. Ask yourself what kind of person is he or she. Do you have anything in common to establish a closer rapport? Perhaps you are both keen on rugby or have an interest in the theatre. Does he, or has he reason, to have confidence in your competence and integrity? What can you say or do that will elicit the response that you require? Bear in mind that you yourself are under scrutiny and must inspire that trust and confidence.

Here again we return to that most important section of a presentation: *know* your client. Identify the need of your prospect, bearing in mind his or her very individual concerns. What exactly is his or her profession or position in business or in the family? A youngish successful businessman for whom things are going very well may feel confident that they will go even better. He may feel, justifiably or not, that he can look after his money better than any way you can suggest, that he does not need your advice. You may well have assessed, however, that he is justifiably conscious of life's relative fragility on this planet and consequently of his own mortality; or you make him aware of it. You can make him aware, if he isn't already, that his progress from strength to strength also depends on his good health and make a case for permanent health insurance. A newly divorced woman with two children who has recently gone back to teaching after an absence of many years, and taken on a mortgage, would understandably be acutely conscious of what the financial future holds for her in old age. She will readily be made aware that she can and should rapidly make up all those lost years' pension contributions.

It all adds up to having a clear idea of who exactly you need to communicate with and knowing as much as you possibly can about that person in the time available, both as a person and regarding the issues directly involved. In our case these are finding out and addressing the prospect's financial planning concerns in the light of his needs and interests. This then is the second essential component of effective communication. Identify your correct target audience.

SELLING LIFE ASSURANCE AND FINANCIAL PRODUCTS

Formulate the right message or approach
Once you are clear as to the result or response that you want to achieve and know the exact party towards whom you need to direct your efforts, you then need to complete the basic package required for achieving the desired result. You do this by adopting and formulating the correct approach that will lead to your desired result. This is the clearly thought-out, carefully chosen sentence that serves as the core, the foundation, as well as the stimulus that leads to acceptance of your message, and enables you to reach your objective. The delivery of this core sentence, as pointed out before, should not take longer than about a half a minute. This most crucial component of your communication package must have the effect of shaking up the other party's thoughts and emotions, and pointing them in the direction you want.

Keeping in mind at all times your listener's needs and interests, the core statement must be one around which you can build your case. It must be one that you can expand upon by adding related statements relevant to your case. Here are some examples relevant to selling financial products:

- *Salesperson's objective*: to persuade customer to take out term assurance. 'In addition to giving peace of mind, term assurance is dirt cheap for non-smokers of your age.' The approach adopted here is peace of mind and cheapness of the product, the implication being that it is hardly worth it *not* to take it up.
- *Salesperson's objective:* to sell free-standing additional voluntary contribution plan. 'You are currently paying 6 per cent of your income towards your pension. You can pay up to a further 9 per cent of your income towards your pension *and* receive tax relief at your top rate. It depends on how comfortable a retirement you want.' The approach here is stressing the need to ensure a comfortable retirement (and highlighting tax relief).
- *Salesperson's objective:* same as above. 'Why give it to the taxman if you can save it instead for retirement?' The approach here stresses the opportunity for and the importance of tax relief.
- *Salesperson's objective:* to sell permanent health insurance

(after, say, one month's deferment). 'You will be paid an income for as long as it takes in the event of illness – yes up to potential retirement if necessary. At your age one is more likely to become ill than die.' The approach here points out the all-embracing nature of the protection cum security the cover provides, and the second sentence the importance of having the cover.

- *Salesperson's objective:* to sell an executive pension plan. 'You don't need to pay. The company can pay and set it off against corporation tax.' This points out that it needn't cost *him* anything, but he benefits from the pension (he, too, can of course contribute up to 15 per cent of his earnings if he wishes).
- *Salesperson's objective:* to sell a personal equity plan. 'Show me any other lump sum investment that is free of all tax on dividends and capital gains, *and* which you can draw out without limit on the time that you need to hold it.' This highlights the opportunity of such tax concessions on an investment.

A well thought-out approach points and leads you unerringly in the direction of your stated goal.

To sum up so far, the three basic ingredients necessary for effective communication are:

- Clearly define your objective or desired response.
- Identify the correct party (person or persons) to whom you must direct your message and who is (or are) in a position to give you what you want.
- Plan and formulate the precise thoughts, words and sentences that will lead you to your desired result.

Although these are the essential basic ingredients for successfully communicating any point or message, they are not all that is required. We shall next look at some other ingredients required for the complete, effective and interesting communication of your message.

Capture attention
Before we read or listen to anything, we usually require some kind of bait to capture our attention. Newspapers do this in the

form of headlines, both in the paper itself and with the posters pinned to newspaper kiosks intended to arouse interest and lure the passer-by to buying the paper. Such bait, whatever the feelings they are intended to arouse or appeal to, do have one thing in common. They are intended to cause the intended target to sit up and take notice. To want to hear or read more, be it out of curiosity, fascination, outrage, delight, provocation, greed, scepticism, temptation, attraction or any number of other trigger emotions.

In the case of the spoken word, it is necessary to excite the interest trigger in your target audience if what you say is not to go in one ear and out the other; if indeed it goes into any ear at all. We all know people with whom it is a pleasure to talk, where the moment they open their mouths we are all ears. Once they start to talk you are relaxed and attentive; you not only hang onto every word but afterwards remember everything that was said. Such people indeed have influence over their fellow beings, and you can too. For you, the salesperson, this ability is vital, because it affects your efficiency in successfully conveying your message and so earning your livelihood.

Usually the criterion of finding the bait or hook with which to capture attention is to ask yourself:

- Whether it will excite and interest your target listener.
- Whether it relates to his interest in a topic close to his heart.
- Whether it conforms to the direction or approach you have adopted for conveying your message.
- Whether it is suitable as the initial stage of your message (it could, for example, be serious, humorous or provocative).

In determining what bait or hook to use, you can use a statement or questions, depending on which is more effective in gaining attention. Good salespeople in fact very often use a question as bait because people usually pay attention when asked something. Here are some examples of baits or interest-provoking comments. They include questions as well as statements relevant to our own special perspective of selling:

- 'Do you intend to rely on the state pension alone when you retire?'
- 'Do you really think that life assurance would be a multi-billion pound business if it served no purpose?'
- Again, for someone who tells you he doesn't believe in life assurance: 'It has its uses.' This is very thought-provoking and leads you on to state your case.
- 'I can help you plan to meet school fees.'
- 'We could get you a much better return on your money than simply placing it in a building society.'
- 'I can ensure that you have a more than adequate income, for as long as you are unable to work due to ill health.'
- 'Will you allow me to undertake a detailed factfind of your circumstances before I make any recommendations?'
- 'Most of the life assurance industry's energies are devoted to successfully investing and managing people's hard-earned savings. If it's good enough for them, it's good enough for me.'

If you always bear in mind the need to use a specific initial word or sentence to capture attention, a little prior thought will often throw up one or two openers for you. The very process of deliberately gaining attention will then become a habit.

Your subject matter
You have adopted your chosen approach, and you have gained your listener's attention. You now need to state your case and prove your point. You must now convey the theme and *substance* of your message.

If you used a question to gain attention you now have to answer it convincingly to make your point. You also need to make clear what you expect of your audience and why. A charity appeal, for example, needs to successfully highlight its cause and make clear the reason your contribution will make a difference to alleviating the problem it is tackling. One such charity notably captures attention by showing a picture of a blind man from a third world country; it goes on to explain that he and thousands like him are blinded by cataracts, which an operation costing *a few pence* donated by members of the public can successfully treat.

SELLING LIFE ASSURANCE AND FINANCIAL PRODUCTS

Even after adopting the correct approach and capturing attention, you will not get your message across unless you know what you are talking about. You must know your subject well – the facts, reasons, relevance, applicability and all – in order to present succinctly and convincingly. Let us look at an example of this in our own field of selling financial products:

'How would you like to increase your pension by say 50 per cent per annum, and enjoy a more comfortable retirement? You can invest up to a further 9 per cent of your income into a pension plan on top of your company's scheme and avoid paying tax on it.' Alternatively, say: 'Avoid paying tax on up to a further 9 per cent of your income by investing it in a pension scheme. You can do this by making free-standing additional voluntary contributions and receive tax relief at the top rate of tax you pay. The sooner you start, the bigger the pension. May I give you an illustration?'

In this example we know our objective, we know our listener and we know the approach to adopt. We capture attention with a question and then convey the substance of the message. We have told the listener in a nutshell what he can do and why he should do it. All in a timespan of about half a minute. What we said will have been understood and digested.

The challenge of the telephone
The telephone can provide your best challenge for putting verbal communication skills into practice. People will be more willing to speak to you over the telephone if they realise that you are brief, get to the point and don't go on for ever. As a salesperson you are on delicate ground. You don't have more than half a minute or so to make your mark, to grab the other person's attention and make your point. Hence the bait or peg for gaining attention is more important than ever. You have only a few seconds to attract and hold your listener's attention and make your point or state your message. It is essential therefore that you are especially well prepared before you make a sales call. Grab the prospect's attention, make your point and ask for an appointment. Remember you know best the benefits that your services can confer on the prospect. You are therefore on at least

equal, and often stronger, ground for gaining an appointment to explain your point more fully (which should be part of the message, anyway) than he is to refuse it. Let us take an example.

'Good morning, Mr X. My name is John Fletcher of Sun Star. We can help you protect your business against loss of profits arising from the death of key employees. The cost is allowable as a business expense. The scheme needs to be individually tailored and obviously provides valuable protection. May I make an appointment to fill you in?'

In this example we have:

Objective:	to make an appointment.
Approach:	protection.
Subject:	keyman assurance.
Bait:	cost offset against tax as a business expense.
Closing:	with a request for an appointment.

Your telephone message must therefore be carefully planned and constructed with supplementary messages for possible reactions that you may encounter. A telephone call is still a two way affair. Once you have made your point you may well be faced with questions. Here again your replies should be brief (under thirty seconds), concise and interesting enough to invite the response you want.

If the person you are trying to reach is not available, leave a brief message rather than letting the secretary and boss wonder, who called. This message should be a constructive one: it should make clear who called and imply that it is to the benefit of the intended listener to return the call.

The communication close: asking for and getting what you want
Whether by phone or in the presence of a prospective client, your message should end with the final part of your attempt to achieve your objective. This is to obtain the response you set out to obtain. You therefore expressly or by implication need to request or demand that response, which may be in the form of an action or a reaction.

An action response will involve acquiescence to a reasonable and persuasive message from you, followed by a strong suggestion or urging to undertake your recommended course of action.

SELLING LIFE ASSURANCE AND FINANCIAL PRODUCTS

A reaction response often results from the gentle persuasion skills discussed earlier in Chapter 7. It is the response that you seek by using the power of suggestion and example. This triggers the desired emotion and it is especially important in selling. In our profession this is the prospect's desire to take up a financial product. The salesperson may say, 'It only costs £32.35 per month for £150,000 life cover over twenty years (for a thirty-one-year-old non-smoker). Given the peace of mind it provides it's very cheap, isn't it? For this reason term assurance is extremely popular.'

This last portion of your message, where you are in effect asking for what you want of your listener and eliciting your desired response is the most crucial segment of your message. Without it the overall effort and opportunity to obtain what you seek is wasted. This is the *close*! If you don't ask for what you want then you will not get it. Shilly-shallying, circumlocution or beating about the bush will result in wasted opportunity.

Your close should result in an expectation of a clear, positive step on the part of your listener. You have identified a need. By his comments or demeanour your listener has acknowledged that need. The product and benefits that you explained are clear to him. You are now entitled to request and expect a response. 'One hundred and fifty thousand pounds of cover rising at 7 per cent a year is reasonable, wouldn't you say? I presume you are happy with that amount, which with non-smokers' discount is even cheaper. Good, let's take down details of your health and I'll keep you informed of progress.' You are demanding action here, within a situation where you have created a flow of minds towards the same conclusion. These techniques apply to many other situations, whether in selling or board meetings – or social situations, as in man to woman in a crowded room, 'Isn't it smoke-filled and noisy in here? Let's adjourn for a quiet drink across the road at the Savoy.'

In our field of selling financial products we want no hint of hard selling. Our methods of closing will usually amount to a courteous suggestion or urging to take up our recommended course of action, or a reaction to the way we put across our message through the use of anecdotes and the power of suggestion. Whatever approach you use depends on the situation and the way that your message is constructed, as part and parcel of your conversation. In this context it is important not to lose control of the flow and logical sequence of your interview, and ensure everything from facts and client concerns to explanation of benefits comes out in good time.

Once you have identified your prospect's needs, be clear in your objective, know your prospect and how best that prospect will be satisfied. You then base your close in the light of this knowledge.

Express yourself powerfully and imaginatively
Whatever the message that you want to communicate, your words must be chosen carefully, creatively and imaginatively to excite the listener's imagination as well as powers of reason. In selling especially, one has to appeal to listeners' emotions as much as to their judgement and logic: but above all the message must be truthful and leave no credibility gap. A positive response needs the successful harnessing of these factors.

Appealing successfully to listeners' emotions can be done by drawing attention to concerns about their family's financial wellbeing and the desire to ensure its continuity at all times, resulting in peace of mind, or it can be concern for provision in sickness or old age. It is this harnessing of emotion with issues close to the listener's heart – provided the cold details also appeal to his mind – that is the spur to action. If the rational element of your message takes the same direction, then you will get the response you want. Would it be more sensible to take a cheaper policy now, given an increase in mortgage interest rates? Perhaps it would be better to take up lower PHI cover or make lower pension contributions until one's immediate financial prospects become clearer. If the client moves, he might need money for additional interest payments. When these practical and rational considerations are in harness with the emotional, both responding to your message, then you have a close, provided that you have established *credibility*. To persuade you must be, and, be seen to be, knowledgeable as well as of the highest integrity.

Even though you are knowledgeable in your subject, choose simple uncomplicated words: and sentences that conjure up a clear picture that your audience can comprehend and appreciate. That is why I earlier stressed clarity and lucidity. Examples and anecdotes used to illustrate a point are powerful tools in communication, because they enable a listener or prospect to identify with the experience of others.

As mentioned before, there should be a logical order to the *manner* in which you convey your overall message. Each point should build on the previous one you have made. The overall message is then received and appreciated in its entirety as well as understood in its constituent parts.

Answering questions: an opportunity not to be missed
In our business, and any other business for that matter, you are bound to be asked questions by those who are taking an interest in what you say. Answering questions presents a great opportunity to reinforce points relevant to the issue and reassure clients as well as presenting an opportunity to make fresh allied points.

Whatever else you go on to say, you first need to answer questions concisely and truthfully. You can then go on to make your own further point if you wish. Why do you think politicians subject themselves to questioning by professional journalists as well as members of the public? The skill lies in answering the question put to you but then using the opportunity presented to get across your own further message.

Question: 'How can I be sure £150 monthly is going to give me a pension of £28,000 a year from age 60? What guarantees are there?'

Answer: 'The projection is based on a 13 per cent return on the underlying fund. The company has a superb investment track record – in fact, well in excess of this figure, but there are *no* guarantees. That is why I urge you to contribute as much as you possibly can, up to 17.5 per cent of your gross income. You need to give yourself the best possible chance of a comfortable retirement.'

You have answered this question brutally and honestly. No messing, and you have taken the opportunity to go on and make a legitimate case for the greatest possible contributions.

HOW TO COMMUNICATE EFFECTIVELY

Question: '£25 per month, for £1,520 per month income after a deferment of six months? Rather expensive isn't it?'

Answer: 'No, it's very cheap, given the peace of mind. One is more likely to fall ill than die.'

You've got your own associated point in with the second sentence, after answering the question with the first.

The skill lies in answering the question and using a connecting sentence to make your own point also. Some further examples:

'I agree with you, and what is more...'

'Yes, it's not cheap, but look how much more expensive it's going to be two years from now – even assuming the rates stay the same.'

'I agree the return at age 60 for that contribution doesn't look spectacular. Look how much less it would be if you defer action for a year.'

'You are the best judge of that (say, of what he can afford). But what I can assure you of, however, is this...' (give assurance).

The lesson is this: questions from your audience are an aid to communication. They further the process and help clear the pathways. They clarify and reinforce your messages, as well as presenting opportunities to add further relevant ones. So welcome them.

Voice control

Your voice is a powerful tool in communication. The way you project it can have a direct influence on your listener's response to what you say. It is affected by your emotional state as well as the conscious effort you make in the way that you use it.

Tension may be reflected in your voice, which can come across as shrill or too fast. Also avoid speaking in a monotone. All this can leave your audience irritable, uncomfortable and less likely to pay attention. Make a conscious effort therefore to adjust the tone of your voice by varying its pitch for the right inflection. Keep down your volume while maintaining your voice and diction audible and clear. Low key makes for greater impact and credibility. Deliver your words at the right pace and speed, according to your message and its recipient.

A good way of strengthening or regaining your listener's attention, heightening his curiosity or assessing the impact of what you are saying, is to pause for one or two seconds. 'How good is it?' – pause – 'It's the best available that I can advise'. Look directly at your listener. The pause catches his attention and heightens interest in the message. You can also emphasise an important part of a message if you speak the last few words softly. This causes the listener to pay extra attention in order to catch what you are saying. In our example you can further strengthen the impact of the second sentence if, after the pause, you were to speak more softly.

The importance of listening

I have already referred to the importance of listening carefully to your prospect. The importance of listening, of paying careful attention to what is said, and the fact that without it one cannot communicate effectively, is not always appreciated; after all, it takes two to tango. Unless the other party believes that what he has to say is being heard and assimilated, that person will not be responsive to your message.

Keep silent when a prospect is talking to you. Maintain eye contact. Pay sympathetic attention. Make it obvious that you are doing so by gentle nodding that implies sympathetic understanding. Reinforce this with occasional phrases like 'I understand ' or 'I see what you mean'.

Incidentally, as was once pointed out to me by a master salesman of financial products, you should also nod gently and affirmatively when you are yourself stating an important fact or making a significant point. This helps to reinforce your message and the chance of acceptance. Such behaviour falls within the realm of body language, which we discuss below.

When listening, do not get offended or emotionally involved in what the other party is saying, even if you perceive it as a criticism of you or your product. The best way of spoiling your chances of eventually getting your message across successfully is to contradict directly or respond angrily to what is being said. Stay calm, composed and maintain eye contact. In fact, pay special attention to the substance of what is being said so that you can respond legitimately and tactfully when it is your turn to speak. Do not interrupt until the other party finishes. However, if you do feel absolutely compelled to interrupt, then soft-pedal and change to a much lower gear with a softly spoken comment such as 'Come now, I understand what you say, but I think it's a little unfair'. Then state your own case while accommodating the other person's feelings. Also look out for signals, especially buying signals, couched in the form of criticism. These are especially useful pointers to a listener's degree of interest and ultimate commitment to your message.

Non-Verbal Communication and Body Language
I have already referred to certain manifestations of body language in previous sections of this book. The whole field of body language is still relatively new, but is an area of constant research. In so far as the financial products salesperson is concerned, some knowledge of the relevant basic principles will help to assess the feelings, motives and sincerity behind what people say or do. Our body language is often a portrayal of what we really think and feel. There are some excellent books on body language (see bibliography) which the reader may like to consult since this section cannot cover the subject fully. Beware, however, of getting carried away into thinking of yourself as an amateur psychologist or body language expert, or exaggerating its importance. It is after all an imprecise subject. It is useful, but it will not by itself help you sell.

Personal space
We earlier discussed the importance of how to position yourself in relation to a prospect during your meeting. Related to this is the question of personal space. Every person has a zone of up to around half a metre that is reserved only for those with whom one has an intimate relationship, such as spouse and family. This space must not be breached during a meeting, or else you may find the other person backing away. The correct space between people at business meetings should be about 1.25 metres, with the correct positioning as discussed earlier.

The eyes
According to the experts, the pupil of the eye will dilate in the event of interest or approval but constrict with lack of interest or disapproval. This of course applies to social as well as business situations. If a prospect feigns lack of interest by appearing distant, silent or aloof his pupils may indicate otherwise. Here again, don't get too carried away because the degree of light also affects pupil size: bright light will cause the pupils to contract, whereas relative darkness causes them to dilate.

Sitting and posture
A more important manifestation of body language for financial product salespeople is the way a prospective customer sits. This can reflect their attitude, positive or negative, to you and your message. In my experience a prospect who is relaxed, interested and paying attention tends to move his neck, head and possibly upper body just slightly forward, even if he is sitting comfortably in an armchair and not around a table. On the other hand, a prospect whose attitude is negative or lacks interest may well lean back into his chair and fold his arms, like a child who doesn't feel like playing, but if he does so in a chair that has no arms it may simply mean that he is more comfortable that way – so use your judgement and make allowances. Such an attitude may also reflect nervousness or insecurity in your presence, or even scepticism. Also, tension can be shown by clenched fists.

If the prospect is obviously paying attention and taking part in the discussion, and then suddenly folds his arms it may mean that he has become doubtful of, or disagrees with, a point you've just made. It is worth reflecting on what you have just said and checking out his reaction. Conversely, if a prospect sitting with arms folded suddenly opens them and leans forward, this would generally indicate sudden interest.

It is not necessarily always the case that folded arms indicate lack of interest or a negative attitude. What is more significant is a sudden change of posture, say, to folded arms indicating negative feelings or unfolding them indicating interest and positive feelings. In this context, if you are in the presence of a husband and wife who turn toward each other to consult in your presence, you should politely fall silent, fold your arms and possibly lean back as an expression that you are temporarily taking a back seat in the discussion and giving them the floor. When they then turn to talk to you again, unfold your arms and lean forward as a gesture that you are available again for discussion.

A prospect who suddenly crosses one leg over another and starts to shake it, while simultaneously tapping his fingers on the armrest, is probably indicating that he is getting nervous or irritable. It could be that you are insisting too forcefully upon a point with which the prospect disagrees or is not certain. It could also mean that you are generally exerting too much pressure. Such pointers indicate that you should immediately start to soft-pedal. In this context also, keep in mind the principles discussed in Chapter 7 on the skills of persuasion.

Untruths

There are certain movements of the hand to the area of the face that indicate someone is probably not telling the truth or not being entirely honest. Such hand movements can accompany a verbal response to a direct question. They include moving the hand to touch or scratch the face, hair, nose, neck or earlobe, or rubbing the eye. Lack of candour can also be revealed by a person suddenly breaking eye contact at the point of response and staring elsewhere, such as the floor or ceiling.

All these are useful pointers to be aware of, especially when they complement your own judgment, but do not view them as hard and fast rules. After all, a person may genuinely have an itchy nose or be visually distracted by something.

If you adhere to the principles outlined here you will be able to communicate much more effectively. These are skills indispensable to our profession of selling financial products and services. You will be able to make your point and convey any message successfully. You will also be able to explain and clarify any matter lucidly and succinctly so that your audience comprehends exactly what you say, in context, and without risk of misunderstanding. Neither hopefully will you bore the pants off anybody.

Effective communication means that you know exactly what you want to say, who you should say it to, how to gain attention, how to say it and ensure that the intended recipient has received and digested the intended message. The key is to be always conscious of the rules when you are communicating. This way you instil into yourself a self-correcting process whereby you will notice when you are not communicating as efficiently as you should.

When I was at junior school we had the most marvellous English teacher. He used to ask us to describe, among other things, various objects in an attempt to stimulate our thinking and develop our powers of expression. I remember, on one occasion, he asked us to describe a sail. Someone responded that it was a white piece of cloth, whereupon he took out and waved his handkerchief and said, 'So is this, try again.' Eventually he was satisfied with 'It is a very large triangular piece of canvas attached to a boat's mast that creates wind resistance and pushes the boat forward.' He was not looking for any great powers of vocabulary. He was simply helping us to achieve and apply clarity of thought to the spoken word. That has to be the aim. As I mentioned at the beginning of this chapter, you can apply the same principles to all situations where you need to communicate successfully, and especially to the selling of financial products.

10
Reflections and Tips On Our Profession

One of the great strengths of our industry is that it is among the most flexible in accommodating and responding to changes and fluctuations in the economic and financial climate. Whatever this climate, your sales production should not be affected to the point where you find yourself struggling. Over the last twenty years in the UK we have seen the stock market dives of 1974 and 1987, high unemployment, high interest rates and more than one recession. Do not fall into the trap of blaming such economic circumstances for consistently poor sales performance on your part. There will always be fluctuations in the relative economic fortunes of any nation.

No matter what the state of the economy, whether it be high interest rates or high unemployment, the majority of the population will more than likely be in work, doing their level best to manage and distribute their resources prudently and find suitable media for their savings or capital. Retired people likewise need to be made aware of safe financial havens from which they can generate assured incomes. Your services as a competent financial consultant will always be in demand.

We have already referred in a previous chapter to clients playing safe during periods of restricted cash flow arising from high mortgage interest rates. However, not everybody is either mortgaged to the hilt or has a recent mortgage, which are the main instances when high interest rates cause budgeting problems. In times of high unemployment, distressing and regrettable as this is both for those affected, their families and society, unemployment does and always will affect a *relatively* small proportion of the working population. Furthermore, unemployment or job insecurity more often than not affects a given section of the economy or industry more than others. For example, at the time of writing my clients in the building industry – architects, civil and structural engineers and associated trades – are having a hard time. Such situations and the insecurity engendered by them must be taken into account when discussing the financial position of those who find themselves in similar circumstances.

No matter how tough the going, however, the employed or the self-employed will still be acutely conscious of their exposure due to lack of or inadequate pension provision. All that such people need is help in concentrating their minds and the correct rearrangement of their spending priorities. It is your job to help them do so. Do not therefore fall into the trap of blaming extraneous factors such as the economic climate for continually poor sales performance. Also, do not allow yourself to be conditioned into performing poorly by colleagues who blame their own bad performance on economic or other outside factors. You can do without them and their influence. As far as you are concerned the sky is the limit. Whatever the economic or fiscal climate, your overall production should not be significantly affected, although the *balance* between the various types of business you write may be. For example, there may well be a drop in business from one particular section of the population affected by economic or fiscal circumstances, so you will have to concentrate your attention that much more on the vast remainder, and step up your prospecting to make up for it.

Whatever ignorant and prejudiced people who cannot see beyond their noses may say, our professional services are indispensable to society at all times, good and bad. Although people's needs for financial services will for various reasons vary throughout their lifespan, these needs will not, with remarkably few exceptions, be non-existent or beyond financial reach. In most cases the solution is a reorganisation of financial priorities. The father and husband on a tight budget will appreciate his desperate need for life assurance protection and protection in the event of accident or ill health. The money saved on four less pints of beer per week can give a man in his late twenties £150,000 of life assurance protection for 25 years. Even an unemployed person can buy some life cover with a tiny portion of his modest budget. It is your job to examine

REFLECTIONS AND TIPS ON OUR PROFESSION

your prospect's circumstances and make constructive, beneficial recommendations that will not cause any hardship.

Our profession is not only crucial to the population at large but we are also the lynch-pin upon which the whole financial services (including life assurance) industry stands. All financial products, like all other commercially designed products, need to be sold for the industry to survive and prosper and it is you who do the selling. Without you, and others like you, who come into daily contact with the buying public, everybody – senior management, actuaries, back-up technical and clerical staff or the tea lady – will have to look elsewhere for work. And if you don't sell properly, ultimately, so will you. That is why it will be all smiles, congratulations and encouragement from your manager when you are doing well, but worried looks when things are not going so well for you. If your performance is flagging, the good manager will invite you for a chat in his office or over a drink to analyse and together pinpoint where the problem lies. These private chats are very useful for identifying errors in your performance, whether during prospecting, your meetings with prospective clients, or your presentation. This is where a good manager comes into his own. He will not only help you spot where any problem lies but will help you boost your self-confidence and optimism, especially if he is convinced that you have what it takes to do well and that any problem is rectifiable. If at any time you are worried for any reason, I urge you to take the initiative and ask to discuss your problems with your manager, or, failing that, a sympathetic and experienced colleague.

You can be assured that if the method and diligence of your prospecting and your performance at client meetings are not at fault, then it is unlikely that you have anything to be seriously concerned about: it is probably one of the periodic downward cycles that everybody in our profession has from time to time. You will simply have to ride out the bad patches. Never, never place yourself in a situation where you are desperate to make a sale; desperation will adversely affect your performance. There is little more dispiriting and likely to affect performance adversely than to depend on last week's sales for this week's income. Most good principals or employers will make allowances in these cases and advance funds against anticipated commission earnings, or put their salespeople on a basic salary.

Always keep firmly fixed in your mind the conviction that you want to perform, that you can perform, that you will perform, and the realisation that periodic temporary downturns need to be accepted with good grace because, as in so many other professions, it is in the nature of the business.

11
Conclusion

This book has described methods of selling financial products that are sound, effective and ethical. They range from the initial search for potential clients to the gaining of a satisfied client's agreement and final signature. Whatever your individual style of conducting business, there are certain principles that you must adhere to if you want a lucrative and satisfying long-term career selling financial products. These are adhered to by all the best and most respected professionals in the field that I have come across over the years, professionals who go about their work with enjoyment and enthusiasm. This should apply equally to you.

There is no doubt that if you follow the principles outlined here you will succeed in what is a financially and socially rewarding profession in which, to a greater extent than most, you are also your own master, with the freedom to plan your time according to the manner that suits you.

In summary, I would put the principal rules for success in selling financial products as follows:

- The correct mental attitude, which is acquired simply by the knowledge and assurance that you can expect success if you follow the right procedures.
- A sufficient depth and breadth of knowledge of financial planning to enable you to assess correctly a prospective client's position and make the right recommendations.
- The necessity to prospect for clients in a disciplined manner and motivate prospects to agree to an interview. Set aside sufficient time to contact both new prospective clients as well as existing ones, and stick to your schedule. Without this nothing happens. Business rarely drops into your lap.

- An efficient factfinding exercise that identifies prospects' needs and enables prospects to recognise those needs.
- Presentations that clearly and convincingly set out the measures that prospects should take and the relevant resulting benefits that they can expect to meet their needs and solve their problems.
- Sensitivity to potential clients' feelings and personality in order to create a good mutual rapport and to appreciate better their concerns and priorities relevant to the subject matter under discussion.

Finally, I wish you the very best of luck!

Appendix

Legislation and Compliance Rules Relating to the Sale of Financial Products

Your work as a financial products salesperson must be conducted within the parameters set out by law. The principal item of legislation is the Financial Services Act 1986 (FSA) and the amendments to it. This Act makes it a criminal offence to carry on investment business without authorisation or exemption. The Act gives powers to the Secretary of State for Trade and Industry, who delegates a great many of these powers to the Securities and Investments Board (SIB) (though they can be taken back if seen fit). The Board in turn has the power, in consultation with the Secretary of State, to recognise self-regulatory organisations, and it has the duty to supervise these organisations (and other bodies) which are largely the source of authority to carry on investment business.

It has been announced that the government has decided to transfer responsibility for financial services from the Department of Trade and Industry to the Treasury, in order to bring the UK into line with practice in other European countries. The FSA will now become the responsibility of the Economic Secretary to the Treasury. However, the DTI will retain responsibility for the supervision of insurance, including life assurance companies, as well as deregulation, general competition policy, insolvency and business audits.

In order to carry on any kind of investment business, a firm or individual needs to be authorised by one of the self-regulatory organisations or authorised directly by the SIB or, in exceptional cases, be exempt. This applies only to the sale and marketing of all life assurance policies, including unit-linked

SELLING LIFE ASSURANCE AND FINANCIAL PRODUCTS

savings plans, insured pension contracts (pension plans), collective investments (unit trusts), PHI, etc. As someone selling such products you will either need to be authorised yourself by one of the SROs (especially if you are running your own firm), or be a registered, appointed representative or employee (i.e. an exempt person) of a principal firm that is authorised. An appointed representative must have a contract for services with a clearly identified principal, authorised under the Act, who is accountable for the investment business carried out by that person. A sales representative of a manufacturing product group who is, say, employed by a life office or has a personal contract of services with it, is also called a company representative.

The profession is polarised: you may be an independent intermediary or the registered appointed representative of one, able to arrange for clients the financial products of a large number of different companies; alternatively, you may be a tied agent-appointed representative (or employee or company representative of such a tied agent) of one particular company, allowing you to sell only the range of products of that company or group. Whichever the case, you will be authorised by or represent a company authorised by the relevant SRO or directly by the SIB. In the case of an independent intermediary the authorising SRO will usually be the Financial Intermediaries, Managers and Brokers Regulatory Association (FIMBRA). As such, your firm will belong to a certain category of membership allowing you to sell at least products among the range previously mentioned. A FIMBRA member is the agent of the client.

On the other hand, where one sells the products of only one marketing group as a tied agent (appointed representative) or employee/representative of such agent, the financial marketing group or life company will be authorised and regulated by the Life Assurance and Unit Trust Regulatory Organisation (LAUTRO). As the name implies, this regulates life assurance companies, unit trust groups, as well as friendly societies (who have to register with the SIB or LAUTRO) in respect of their retail marketing of life assurance products, pension plans and unit trusts. Apart from SROs, certain recognised professional bodies, such as the Law Society for solicitors or one of the Accountancy bodies, can be granted recognition by the SIB.

APPENDIX

They may authorise their respective members to carry on investment business in addition to their professional role where that business constitutes a small proportion of their work.

Moves are currently afoot with a view to creating a single SRO to regulate both the independent and tied/manufacturing product sectors of the financial services industry dealing with the private client retail sector. This is referred to in more detail later in this Appendix.

You need to be clear as to which SRO you or the company that you represent derives its authority from, and also into which category of membership you and your firm (if an IFA and FIMBRA member) are placed. As a possible independent financial adviser and FIMBRA member, your firm's category of membership may restrict it to permission to advise upon and sell life assurance, pension plans, unit trusts and the like, but forbid it, and therefore also yourself, to handle clients' money. To allow it to do so would require a different category. Straying outside the authorised category can lead to committing a criminal offence.

You therefore need to make sure that you comply with all the rules of your regulatory body. You also need to establish exactly what your relationship is with your firm. You could, for example, be working for yourself as a sole trader or be a director or employee of your firm. You could be the appointed representative of a firm that is authorised and takes responsibility for the way you conduct your business, as would be the case if you were the company representative of a life assurance company or product manufacturing group. If so, there must be a suitable contract between you and your principal firm that places an obligation on you to act responsibly during the course of your work. As is the case with any other appropriate regulator, if you are the appointed representative of an independent financial intermediary authorised by FIMBRA you need to be registered yourself. This involves applying for such registration. The forms involved for this are detailed, and there are stringent requirements to ensure suitability, including a demand for references, before you will be accepted. You need to be 'fit and proper' – which means honest, solvent and competent – as indeed does anyone who seeks authorisation with an SRO. Such a registered appointed representative has a contractual relationship with the authorised principal firm. The principal firm undertakes to comply with the rules of the regulatory body and takes responsibility for the investment activities of the appointed representative (or employee) who is in contact with the investing public.

Do therefore make sure that you understand and operate within the guidelines of your particular SRO. There is no substitute for consulting your SRO's rulebook or, assuming that you are an appointed representative, seeking guidelines from your employers or principals who are obliged to ensure that you comply and will provide you with the appropriate compliance guide. You will also be provided with the relevant documents that you may need to hand to the client or that need to be completed and signed by both of you (see references to Buyer's Guide and Terms of Business letter below).

The Act also makes it a criminal offence for anyone other than an authorised person or firm to issue, or cause to be issued, an advertisement in the UK unless its contents have been approved by an authorised person, or it falls within one of the exempted categories. For this reason anybody approving an advertisement on behalf of an authorised firm must ensure proper understanding of the rules of the SIB or the relevant self-regulatory organisation. An investment advertisement in this respect is any advertisement which invites the public to enter into an investment agreement. You must therefore ensure that any advertisement you place or mailshot you undertake using your firm's name and letterhead has been scrutinised and approved by the firm responsible for you. Advertisements that invite 'off the page purchase' must be restricted to life policies, unit trusts and PEPS. The SIB provides a list of questions which it is considered reasonable to expect a purchaser to be able to answer for him or herself after studying the advertisement.

The concept of polarisation referred to earlier means that the private client should be clear about the legal capacities of the firm and individual with whom he or she is doing business, i.e. who is acting as agent for whom. An independent intermediary should present himself as, and is deemed to be acting as, agent of the client/investor. The representative of a company that brings out products by definition acts on behalf of that

APPENDIX

company. Both are required to give *best advice* within the confines of their respective roles.

The basic principle of polarisation is illustrated by the fact that according to the SIB 'employees or appointed representatives of product companies who are authorised to canvass for business, are not allowed, and must be prohibited either by the contract governing their activities or by a specific restriction empowered by Section 44(4) and (5) of the Act, from canvassing for or advising about life policies or unit trusts emanating from outside the marketing group'. (Marketing group refers to the life company or financial group responsible for bringing out the above-mentioned products.)

However, not only is the concept of best advice referred to above under scrutiny, with the emphasis moving toward giving good advice or suitability to the needs and circumstances of the client, but the duty of best advice upon independent financial advisers differs from that expected of tied agents. The IFA's duty is to recommend to the client the best product available to meet his needs as a result of monitoring a reasonable number of product companies. He should take into account factors such as price, the financial strength of the product company, importantly their investment performance and their overall efficiency. The best advice responsibility of a tied agent is to recommend the product of the tied agent's manufacturing product group that best meets the need of the client. If the tied agent's product group does not have a suitable product that meets a client's needs, a tied agent may introduce the client to an independent financial adviser and be paid for the introduction. He is not, however, allowed to introduce the client to another product manufacturing/marketing group which may have a suitable product, nor to any of its tied agents.

Although this Appendix is not intended to be detailed or comprehensive, I would nevertheless like to bring to your attention certain SRO rules of particular importance relating to the conduct of business. The regulatory bodies have similar rules that must, according to their rulebooks, afford client investors at least equivalent protection to that provided by the SIB rules.

You should always make clear the nature of your relationship with your client. This is done by handing the prospect a Buyer's Guide at the very beginning of any meeting. Its content

SELLING LIFE ASSURANCE AND FINANCIAL PRODUCTS

and format is set out by the relevant regulatory body. The guide explains the basis of the intermediary's relationship with the client, including the intermediary's obligations towards that client. It explains the client's rights, distinguishes between an independent intermediary and a representative of a particular product company or tied agent and points out which the salesperson/adviser represents. It also points out that the intermediary is bound by the rules of the relevant SRO. It should make clear, for example, that if you are an authorised independent intermediary (or registered representative of such an intermediary) you can select the most suitable product from the range of the companies available on the market. It should also make clear that you and/or the firm you work for will receive commissions from the company whose products you may have sold. It should also specify that you have a duty to explain the main features, costs and potential future benefits of the product that you recommend. It must advise the client of whether he has a right to change his mind before he commits himself to buying the particular product, plus any costs incurred in doing so. He should be aware that if he does change his mind, in some cases he may not get back all that he paid if investment values have fallen. Finally, it should inform the client that information relating to commission paid, product and other details will be supplied to the client by the product company in writing (see sample Buyer's Guide at the end of this Appendix).

You have a duty to *know your client*. This means taking reasonable steps to ascertain correctly his or her personal and financial circumstances and other relevant details, including the client's financial objectives, assets, liabilities, plus current and anticipated expenses. This involves a proper factfinding exercise. Write down the client's replies to your relevant questions, and after you have completed your business attach a clear report, based on your factfind, of what you have advised and why (which you can attach to the completed factfind information sheet). The factfind and your report should be placed in the client's file for future reference or for possible inspection by the SRO inspector. The rule also requires that you must be satisfied that, having taken all reasonable steps, the client understands the nature and degree of risk that the investment, in the form of the recommended product, is subject to.

APPENDIX

The rules require that you give best advice in determining what is a suitable product for your client in the light of all reasonable steps taken to know your client, and having regard to any other relevant information that you should have known about. You must ensure that your judgements and recommendations are made on a well informed basis. (The situation is different if you are merely executing his instructions – known as an execution-only client – when he enjoys less protection.)

Recommendations must be made with all reasonable care and include enough information to provide a sufficient basis upon which the client can agree to take up a recommendation. You should make sure that you avoid suggesting that returns achieved on investments in the past for products that you recommend will necessarily be achieved in the future. Consistency of past performance, however, can be taken into consideration in assessing likelihood of future performance.

As a result of exceptions to the basic interpretations of section 56 of the Act made by the Secretary of State through the SIB, which appear in the rules of the self regulatory bodies, you may make cold calls provided that they relate to life insurance policies or pension contracts, collective investments such as unit trusts (or unit trust PEPS) or contracts to manage the assets of an occupational pension fund. A cold call is an unsolicited approach such as a personal visit or telephone communication made without express invitation. A cold call may also be made on someone who has expressly consented to such calls being made, as in the case of a person who has responded to an advertisement which makes it clear that a salesman may call as a result.

Anyone making a permitted cold call must do so in a reasonable manner. A call must not be made at an unreasonable hour, i.e. before 9am, after 9pm and all day on Sunday. A call must not be made to an ex-directory number except with the prior consent of the subscriber. Further requirements include:

- The caller must ensure that his or her name, as well as the name of the firm represented, is conveyed to the prospect at the outset, with reminders where necessary.
- The caller must check that it is convenient for the prospect to talk and allow the prospect to terminate the call if the prospect so wishes.

- The caller must make clear the true purpose of the call.
- The caller must be truthful and accurate as to the product or service he wishes to sell.
- The salesperson must provide a telephone number and address through which the prospect can contact the salesperson to cancel or alter any appointment.

If the caller makes an offer which, if accepted, would result in an agreement to invest in or take up a financial product then the consequences of the client's acceptance must be made clear to him. The client must also receive a letter from the product company, usually a member of LAUTRO in the case of the sale of life policies and unit trusts, informing the client of the fourteen-day cooling off period during which time the client can change his or her mind.

Terms of Business Letter
This is the most important document that you should hand to a client before you provide him with any investment service. The terms of Business letter:

- Describes, in the form prescribed, the investment services provided.
- States that the organisation or person is authorised by the regulatory body to provide the services and is bound by its rules.
- States the manner by which the firm is remunerated.
- States either that it is not authorised to handle clients' money in the form of cheques made out to itself or by handling cash, or it states that it is so authorised. If it is, authorised to handle clients' money it gives details of how such clients' money will be handled, the measures taken to ensure its safekeeping, plus the client's right of inspection of his assets and all relevant documents and records. It also mentions that the client's records will be held for seven years (this period may be less in some cases).
- Gives details of any locum arrangements made to look after clients' interests.
- States whether or not it holds professional indemnity insurance.

APPENDIX

You should sign preferably two copies of this document. The client should sign both also under a statement further down to the effect that he has received a copy of the Terms of Business Letter plus a copy of the Buyer's Guide and, if you wish, confirming his agreement to you and your firm acting as his or her financial adviser (see sample Terms of Business letter at the end of this Appendix). Leave one copy of the letter with the client.

If a client purchases a contract in response to an off-the-page advertisement, you need to send a Terms of Business letter only if you subsequently meet or write to him.

Product Disclosure

When you have sold a financial product, the client is entitled to full product disclosure (i.e. to know exactly what he has bought) and you, the salesperson, have to be qualified to provide such disclosure. This must be provided at the meeting or shortly afterwards. You can therefore comply with this obligation by supplying printed product details to the client at the meeting or it can be sent by the product organisation with the cooling off notice. It is also your duty to advise the client what risks, if any, are involved in any course of action he may decide to undertake, as well as point out the advantages and disadvantages of any such course of action.

Competence

As a salesperson, whether tied agent or independent, you can recommend a product only if you are fully competent to advise upon and sell it. This means that you need to be fully conversant with its uses and within its relevant contexts of law and tax, as well as being able to compare it with other competing investment products. One is not allowed to sell a product without first undergoing proper training in it with the results recorded.

Advertising and Publicity

Any advertisements you place must be clear and not misleading. Furthermore, it is a criminal offence to issue or cause to be issued an advertisement relating to investment business in the UK unless it has been approved by an authorised person or it falls within an exempted category. Do make sure, therefore, that the full advertising copy of any mailshot you send out on your own initiative on behalf of yourself and/or your firm has this approval and also complies with the following requirements:

- An advertisement or mailshot must clearly indicate the regulatory body that regulates the firm by, for example, displaying its logo. It must not, however, imply that the regulatory body endorses the advertisement.
- An advertisement must observe all the standards of the Advertising Standards Authority in addition to the rules set out by the regulatory body that controls the firm.
- If the advertisement or mailshot relates to collective investments (e.g. unit trusts) it must also be approved by the trustee or custodian of that scheme.
- A record must be kept of the advertisement content and of the person who approved it.
- The advertisement or mailshot must not be issued with the intention of persuading a prospective client to enter into a different form of investment than the one indicated in the advertisement or mailshot.
- Any advertisement or promotional literature must avoid untrue, out-of-date or misleading statements, statements of opinion not honestly held at the time the advertisement was issued, or any statement of fact that may not be valid during the whole of the time that the advertisement is due to appear.
- Past performance can only be published if its source is quoted, it is relevant to what is advertised and is not exaggerated. It must also be accompanied by the statement that past performance is not necessarily a guide to future performance.
- Words inviting the public to respond to the advertisement have to be in a form acceptable to the regulatory body.

Bear in mind that if you undertake advertising or mailshots, you will be personally responsible to your firm for its compliance with the advertising rules. The advertisement should carry (or there must be available) a statement of the investment business which it has been authorised to conduct.

All advertisements, mailshots and other business communications must state the name, address and telephone number of the firm and the name of the member person within the firm sending it. All business documents, compliance slips, letterheads, business cards, etc., should state the name of the regulatory body that has authorised the firm.

You should ensure that you and your firm keep all necessary records to establish that there has been compliance with the rules relating to all transactions with or on behalf of clients. You and/or your firm must keep copies of any complaint relating to the conduct of business made to you or your firm in writing by or on behalf of a client, as well as keeping records of your and/or your firm's (i.e. member's) written response, together with a record of any action taken in response to such a complaint. A member firm of which you are a part must inform the complainant of his or her right to complain to the regulatory body, which is also obliged to investigate the complaint.

You and your firm must never handle clients' money or assets if you and your firm are not authorised to do so. Assets, within the meaning of the rules, refers to documents of title.

Whether or not your member firm is authorised to hold clients' money or assets depends on the category of business for which it is authorised. If authorised to hold assets, the member firm must comply with the rules about the safe custody of documents relating to clients' assets, and account for them to clients every six months. If not authorised to hold clients' money, you and your firm must never handle cash or accept a cheque made out to your member firm.

If authorised to hold clients' money you and your firm must comply strictly with the rules relating to the holding of such money. Some of the rules relating specifically to clients' money are contained in the Financial Services (Clients' Money) Regulations 1987, derived from Section 55 of the Act.

Any clients' money must be held on trust (or as an agent in Scotland) in a client bank account at an approved bank. Such an account has to be in the name of the firm but must include the word 'client' in its title. Notice must be given to the bank upon the opening of such an account and the bank must acknowledge that the money is held by the firm as trustee (or agent in Scotland). The bank must also acknowledge that it is not allowed to set off against another account of the firm. The client account must not be overdrawn either in total or in respect of any one client. Do therefore make absolutely sure that you are aware of your member firm's authorisation category and status before you accept any monies on behalf of clients to pass on, and do not accept any such monies if your member firm is not so authorised.

You should be aware that your authorised member firm will be subjected to monitoring by periodic random checks carried out by the SRO compliance officers. Visits may also be initiated by receipt of complaints or by the checking of routine reports. The SRO has the right to make such visits unannounced. You should therefore be sure that you yourself are acquainted with, and comply with, all the rules of your SRO relating to your financial advice and sales duties. This includes the proper keeping of up-to-date records and appropriate reports relating to each client and meetings.

Failure to comply with the rules of the SRO by you or your firm, or any misconduct brought to its attention by complaint or inspection, can have serious consequences for you and your firm. This includes the removal of your (an individual's) registration or termination of your authorised firm's membership. Lesser sanctions may involve the imposition of conditions on a firm's membership, a requirement that the member firm remedy any breach that caused disciplinary action to be taken, or result in a reprimand to the member firm.

Amendments to the and Other Recent Developments
As a result of amendments to the FSA by the Companies Act 1989, the SIB has introduced Statements of Principle followed by the introduction of core rules.

The statements of principle
These relate to the following areas of concern and reiterate what should in any case be existing practice:

APPENDIX

- Integrity. A firm should observe high standards of integrity and fair dealing.
- Skill, care and diligence. A firm should act with due skill, care and diligence.
- Market practice. A firm should observe high standards of market conduct. It should also, to the extent endorsed for the purpose of this principle, comply with any code or standard as is in force from time to time and as it applies to the firm either according to its terms or by rulings made under it.
- Information about customers. A firm should seek from customers it advises or for whom it exercises discretion, any information about their circumstances and investment objectives which might reasonably be expected to be relevant in enabling it to fulfil its responsibilities to them.
- Information for customers. A firm should take reasonable steps to give a customer it advises, in a comprehensible and timely way, any information needed to enable him to make a balanced and informed decision. A firm should similarly be ready to provide a customer with a full and fair account of the fulfilment of its responsibilities to him.
- Conflicts of interest. A firm should try to avoid any conflict of interest arising or, where conflicts do arise, it should ensure fair treatment to all its customers by disclosure, internal rules of confidentiality, declining to act, or otherwise. A firm should not unfairly place its interests above those of its customers and, where a properly informed customer would reasonably expect that the firm would place his interests above its own, the firm should live up to that expectation.
- Customer assets. Where a firm has control of, or is otherwise responsible for, assets belonging to a customer which it is required to safeguard, it should arrange proper protection for them, by way of segregation and identification of those assets or otherwise, in accordance with the responsibility it has accepted.
- Financial resources. A firm should ensure that it maintains adequate financial resources to meet its investment business commitments and to withstand the risks to which its business is subject.

- Internal organisation. A firm must organise and control its internal affairs in a responsible manner, keeping proper records, and where the firm employs staff or is responsible for the conduct of investment by others, it should have adequate arrangements to ensure that they are suitable, adequately trained and properly supervised and that it has well defined compliance procedures.
- Relations with regulators. A firm should deal with its regulator in an open and cooperative manner and keep the regulator promptly informed of anything concerning the firm which might reasonably be expected to be disclosed by it.

The core rules

The designated core rules made by the SIB are applicable to all firms of whichever SRO they belong, except members of recognised professional bodies. The purpose behind them is to provide a degree of uniformity of standards. Following from this, it is intended that the SROs will then support and supplant these designated core rules with their own rules, tailored to the activities of the firms or persons they authorise and regulate. The SIB will then be expected to agree that the SRO rulebooks, together with their monitoring and compliance arrangements and procedures, provide sufficient protection to the investing customer public.

The core rules, of which there are forty in total, cover matters relating to the conduct of business by authorised persons, including those directly regulated by the SIB. They will be brought into force for each SRO when each is ready to bring additional (third tier) rules into force. Until such time, the existing SRO rules relating to the conduct of business remain in force.

Some of the areas covered are the way in which new business is sought by authorised firms, the regulation of existing relationships between authorised firms and their existing clients, and the way in which complaints are dealt with:

- Advertising and marketing – i.e. the manner in which new business is sought by authorised firms.

Advertisements must be fair and accurate and must not contain misleading statements. Unsolicited calls will be allowed. The Buyer's Guide is to be renamed the Client's Guide. There are rules for product disclosure. A cooling off period of fourteen days applies to investments which can be sold as a result of unsolicited calls. There are requirements to ensure that a firm's appointed representative is a 'fit and proper person' to act as one, and to control and monitor his conduct of business.
- Inducements. Reasonable steps must be taken to ensure that firms or their agents neither offer or solicit any inducement that conflicts with their duties towards clients.
- Conflict of interest. Where a firm has a material interest in a transaction that gives rise to a conflict of interest, it must not knowingly advise in relation to such a transaction unless it takes appropriate steps to ensure fair and proper treatment for its client.
- Polarisation. The Rules reiterate the requirement that IFAs and product organisations or their marketing arms (or tied agents) stick to their proper assigned roles.
- Customer agreements. The Rules set out terms of customer agreements between authorised firms and their clients. These include rules on how agreements are made, the manner in which instructions are to be communicated and how agreements are to be terminated. A customer agreement is a written agreement to which the customer has assented in writing after having had a proper opportunity to consider its terms.
- Quality and suitability of advice. Transactions advised and arranged must be suitable in the light of the facts both disclosed and of which the firm should already be aware. The Rules stress the need for firms to obtain full information about the products which they may sell, and also that they should not recommend a packaged product if they can recommend another, within their authority to advise upon and sell, which more effectively meets the client's needs.
- Safeguarding client assets. A firm that is authorised to hold client assets must keep them safe. They must be properly recorded and registered.

SELLING LIFE ASSURANCE AND FINANCIAL PRODUCTS

- Compliance and complaints. A firm must operate proper monitoring and compliance procedures and ensure that the regulatory body's rules are obeyed. It must have procedures to ensure that customer complaints are properly handled and, where required, prompt action is taken to remedy any situation. It must also be able to advise clients on how to proceed further with a complaint within the regulatory system. Authorised firms are also required to contribute to a compensation fund set up by the SIB whereby investors may recover up to a maximum of £48,000 if a firm is unable to meet its liabilities in the event of its going into liquidation.

Issues of disclosure
One of three discussion papers published by the SIB relates to the quality and amount of information that should be disclosed to investors buying packaged products. It makes certain proposals, most importantly that the information imparted should be split between key features to be given at the time a product is recommended; important information to be provided no later than the cooling off period, and other useful information upon request only.

In the above respect LAUTRO has correspondingly published its new rules (Bulletin No. 53) on product disclosure (and status disclosure). These new rules mark a further advance in disclosure obligations to a client by clarifying to the client (1) the status of the financial adviser and (2) the key features of the product that a client is buying. The main points of the rules are:

- A new Client's Guide, replacing the Buyer's Guide, will explain the status of the individual advising the prospective client, his duties, who is responsible for him, and by whom he is represented.
- Tied agent firms selling the products of one organisation must make their status clear by putting the following statement on their advertisements and stationery and on notices in their premises. '(Name of firm) represents only (Name of product organisation) for life assurance, pensions and unit trust business'.

APPENDIX

- Salespersons who act for only one product organisation must show clearly on their business cards that they are company representatives of that product-providing organisation.
- When a client investor is advised to buy a regular premium life assurance policy or annuity, this must be followed by a letter explaining the reasons for the recommendation.
- Product information is split into (a) key features which must be handed over before a proposal is signed and (b) important information which must be sent to the investor before or with the cancellation notice.
- Key features specific to the investing client must be available on request.

For the first two years after the rules come into effect the client specific information can include tables of specimen values, but after that the information must be properly specific to the client.

Significantly, the Chancellor of the Exchequer, in response to a report under the Financial Services Act 1986 by the Director of Fair Trading on the marketing and sale of investment-linked life assurance products, announced on July 22nd 1993 that he is issuing directions to the Securities and Investments Board requiring them to develop a new approach to the regulation of the marketing of packaged life assurance products. The SIB will bring forward proposals to rectify the deficiencies identified and to improve the information available to investors buying packaged life assurance policies. According to the Chancellor the decision will improve competition and consumer confidence in the life assurance industry and bring benefits to investors and savers.

Among the required changes are:

- New rules which will give a clear and quantified account of the effect of life offices' intended surrender value practices on the value of the policy if cashed in early beyond the initial five years without implying guaranteed projected values or overloading investors with unnecessary amounts of figures.

- New rules which will require illustrations of projected returns on life assurance policies to use the life offices' own recent charges, and not standard assumptions.
- Adaptation of the best advice regime to allow differential pricing in the tied sector.
- Most importantly from your standpoint as the salesperson, proposals for automatic disclosure of commission in cash terms at an early stage by all distribution channels or equivalent information in the cases of direct sales forces (and bancassurance where commission is not paid).

Following the above, a consultative document was published in January 1994 in which the Securities and Investments Board stated that from January 1995, all financial advisers selling life assurance policies must disclose to the investor at the point of sale the commission they will receive in cash terms before the investor signs anything. Investors will also have to be given more information about other matters such as the surrender values of their policies throughout their term. Also illustrations of future performance must be based on the charges of the individual company rather than the industry charges currently used. Commission tables will also be published.

All the above developments make it even more imperative that you keep yourself up to date on all the compliance rules applicable to yourself, and that you comply with the rules accordingly. If, therefore, you are employed by or are an appointed representative of an authorised firm (or a company representative of a manufacturing product organisation) make sure that you receive proper and regular guidance from those responsible for your conduct of work.

Proposals and Plans for the Establishment of a New Regulatory Body

Following a report in March 1992 by Sir Kenneth Clucas, at the request of the SIB, a formation committee called the Personal Investment Authority was set up with a view to drawing up plans for the establishment of a new single regulatory body

APPENDIX

that would be responsible for regulating all companies' dealings with private investors (i.e. the retail sector). This would merge FIMBRA and LAUTRO and also some of the private sector non-stockbroking responsibilities of the other SROs. The intention currently is, if things go according to plan, to put the new system in place sometime in 1994. An advantage of such a system would be that a single regulator for life assurance, personal pensions and unit trusts is likely to reduce the cost of regulation to companies, thus indirectly reducing the cost to consumers, and also to make monitoring of salespeople easier.

Another issue that such a move is intended to address in the light of increased compensation liabilities encountered by FIMBRA (whose liabilities above a capped figure of £5 million were consequently agreed to be met by LAUTRO members) is the question of who should be responsible for meeting the compensation claim bills of the Investors Compensation Scheme. It is envisaged that all members would be expected to pay their share.

It must be emphasised that the distinction between tied agents and independent financial advisers will continue.

According to a PIA consultative document that came out on September 24th, 1992, and was met with varying degrees of enthusiasm, the Personal Investment Authority (also the agreed name of the proposed new regulatory body) would have a wider regulatory scope than that of either LAUTRO or FIMBRA with the aim of providing a one-step alternative to the current arrangements.

Providers of packaged investment products for private investors would be regulated by the PIA.

The consultative paper said, 'It is intended that only firms which carry on substantial amounts of their business with or for private investors should become members, other firms remaining subject to the existing regulators.

'The PIA would be able to regulate business done for non-private customers where these activities are subsidiary or incidental to a firm's main business. However, some firms may continue to need two regulators.'

There seems to be an implication that some FIMBRA members, such as those whose main business is in corporate

SELLING LIFE ASSURANCE AND FINANCIAL PRODUCTS

finance, would be more appropriately members of the Securities and Futures Authority.

In view of the continually developing nature of the situation it is therefore necessary that you should keep abreast of developments in this and allied matters, through the weekly (and monthly) press for personal financial advisers.

Other Relevant Legislation

In addition to the Financial Services Act 1986 and its Amendments, there are other items of legislation that have a direct bearing on the manner that you should conduct your business activities as a life assurance and financial products salesperson. These include the following:

The Misrepresentation Act 1967

Under this Act a person who enters into a contract after a misrepresentation made to him by the other party and suffers loss as a result, can either rescind the contract or confirm it and then claim damages. This includes innocent and not just fraudulent misrepresentation, unless the person who made it can prove there were reasonable grounds to believe that the facts represented were true. All the more reason therefore that you be well informed, accurate and up to date during your presentations.

The Trade Descriptions Act 1968

This Act makes it a criminal offence for a false or misleading description to be given to services (or goods) during the course of trade. Under the Act it is also an offence 'to give any false indications, direct or indirect, that any goods or services supplied are of a kind supplied to any person'. This means that as a salesperson you cannot claim to have sold a policy to a friend or acquaintance of the prospective client, and claim that the friend or acquaintance was so pleased that he thought the prospective client might also be interested *if such a statement were not true.*

The Insurance Companies Act 1974

Section 63 of this Act states that any person promising or forecasting misleading information or making any reckless claims

APPENDIX

or statements in order to induce another person (prospective client) to enter into any contract of insurance (Life Assurance) shall be guilty of an offence.

The Data Protection Act 1984

Under this Act any individual or organisation, including a life assurance company, financial product provider and financial intermediary, who stores information on computer about living individuals, such as details of clients and policyholders, is required to register with the Data Protection Register together with the reasons for and circumstances under which the data will be used and the person(s) who will use them. Failure to do so may result in penalties.

The Act gives protection to anyone who might have his or her details stored on computer. Provisions in the Act also relate to the conduct of persons maintaining the records and give the right to individuals subject to information held on computer to inspect that information and challenge its accuracy. Such a person may also claim compensation resulting from incorrect data and its use if he has suffered loss.

To assist businesses which provide financial advice or arrange personal investment for individuals, the Data Protection Register has published a Guidance Note (No. 24). Financial product providers and intermediaries, like all computer users under the Act, must comply with the provisions of good practice (see below). For financial advisers whose activities fall within the provisions of the Financial Services Act 1986 and its 'know your customer' rules, it is especially important to comply with the principle that states that 'The information contained in personal data shall be obtained, and personal data shall be processed fairly and lawfully'. Guidance Note 24 provides some guidelines to bear in mind when obtaining information relating to individuals which is to be stored on computer. It also makes specific recommendations on how to apply these guidelines within the context of the requirements of the Financial Services Act, and especially in situations requiring the use of a questionnaire. It aims to help those within the industry to obtain personal data in a manner which provides reassurance for clients while also avoiding any breaches of the law.

SELLING LIFE ASSURANCE AND FINANCIAL PRODUCTS

The other provisions briefly are:

- Stored information about individuals shall not be retained for longer than necessary for the reasons for which it was originally obtained.
- The information should not be excessive. It should be adequate and relevant to the specific purpose of its use.
- The information must not be disclosed to anyone or in any manner not connected with the purpose for which it is kept.
- The information should be up to date and accurate. It should be corrected if properly challenged by the individual who is the subject of the data.
- An individual must be given access to any information relating to him as a result of requests made with not unreasonable frequency.
- The information must be held securely and not easily accessible to anyone who is not authorised to see or handle such information.
- The purpose for which the information is held should be stipulated at the user's registration, and it must be for a specific and lawful purpose.

Anyone not registered under the Data Protection Act and not clear about the position can seek and obtain advice from the Registrar's Office, and would also benefit from reading Data Protection Guidance Note No. 2, 'Insurance Brokers and Consultants – Registration Guidance'. The Guidance Notes, Guidelines on the Data Protection Act itself, registration forms and a leaflet outlining an individual's rights under the Act can be obtained free from:

The Office of the Data Protection Registrar
Springfield House
Water Lane
Wilmslow
Cheshire SK9 5AX
Tel. 0625-535777
Fax. 0625-524510

APPENDIX

The Consumer Credit Act 1974
This Act deals with the form and content of advertisements and quotations for loans and mortgages. You should study the provisions of this Act in detail if you are involved in providing these kinds of financial services (if, for example, you are attached to a building society), so that you are familiar with them, both from the point of view of the consumer as well as the lender or service provider.

The Act includes a requirement for a true Annual Percentage Rate (APR) to be included on all quotations. The lender is also obliged to give the borrower all the relevant details of the agreement and of its operation. Note that the client must receive a copy of the agreement for his own reference when provided with the agreement for him to sign.

Among the provisions of the Act are those that regulate the contents of the agreement, such as the borrower's right of cancellation, if any, including the provision for the cooling-off period if he wishes to change his mind and cancel the agreement.

The Act stipulates the steps which lenders are entitled to take and the procedures that they must follow if they want to enforce the provisions of a loan agreement by demanding full repayment of a loan if a borrower defaults on his repayments. The Act also enables someone who has been refused credit to request from the people who have refused the credit all the information which they hold about him. He is then allowed to take appropriate steps to rectify any incorrect information held about him.

Legislation for Compliance with EC Directive
In order to comply with EC Money Laundering Directive, the UK Parliament has introduced legislation effective from April 1st, 1994, which obliges independent financial advisers to ask new clients doing investment and insurance business to prove their identity by providing passport photographs.

Advisers will need to verify a client's identity if single premium business is over 15,000 Ecus (about £10,000) or if regular premium business is over 1,000 Ecus (about £660).

If a client pays with a cheque drawn on his own account or by direct debit the adviser does not need to make checks.

SELLING LIFE ASSURANCE AND FINANCIAL PRODUCTS

A reference from an accountant, solicitor or a trusted employee is acceptable. If any of these is not available then an adviser must ask a client for a passport photograph plus a utilities bill which shows his address. The evidence must be kept on file for five years.

As in the case of the regulatory body rules, you should keep abreast of legislation affecting your conduct of business by reading the relevant professional press.

These notes are a brief and selective guide only. They are based upon my own personal understanding of the matters referred to and no responsibility is accepted for their accuracy.

FIMBRA Buyer's Guide to:
Life Assurance • Personal Pensions • Unit Trust Products

1. Advisers on life assurance, personal pensions and/or unit trust products are of two types:

Either   Representatives of a particular company

Or   Independent

Both types of adviser should only recommend life assurance, personal pensions or unit trust products if they consider such a product suitable to your needs.

2. A representative of a particular company acts **on its behalf** and will recommend a product picked only from the range of those offered by that particular company.

3. Your adviser is **independent**. He (or she) will **act on your behalf** in recommending a product picked from the range of all the companies that make up the market place. Unless you come to some other arrangement with him, your adviser (or the firm he works for) will normally receive commission from the company that issues the life policy or units to you. You will be given details of this commission by the company paying it, and if you ask him, by your adviser.

4. Your adviser is bound by the rules of FIMBRA (The Financial Intermediaries, Managers and Brokers Regulatory Association) which have been designed for your protection. They require that:

APPENDIX

• Your adviser must explain the main features of the product he is recommending to you, and should help you to understand the risks there may be and the costs there will be as well as the potential future benefits you could gain from it.

• Your adviser must tell you whether you have a right to change your mind before you commit yourself to buying the product. If you do change your mind, in some cases you may not get back all that you paid if investment values have fallen. Be sure to ask your adviser about any right to change your mind, and any cost you might incur by doing so.

5. The company whose product you buy will give you the following information in writing:

• Full details of the product, including how you pay, how much and for how long; its benefits to you; and, for certain types of product, an indication of the company's expenses or charges that will be taken out of the money you pay. These expenses or charges may arise both at the time you first buy the product and also in the future.

• Details of the commission payable to your adviser (or the firm he works for). This commission will form part of the company's expenses or charges.

• An indication, where your investment is a life policy, of how much money, if any, you would receive if you stop the policy within five years of taking it out.

6. **Note carefully:** If you want more information now about any of these matters, or if anything else is not quite clear to you, tell your adviser. It is his job to help you understand everything you want to know.

7. Issuing this guide is a requirement of FIMBRA, Hertsmere House, Hertsmere Road, London E14 4AB. Telephone 071-538 8860, 071-895 1229

SELLING LIFE ASSURANCE AND FINANCIAL PRODUCTS

Sample Terms of Business Letter

A FIMBRA Member

Your own letterhead

Name and address
of client

Date

Dear [Name of Client]

TERMS OF BUSINESS LETTER

ABC Limited is authorised by the Financial Intermediaries Managers and Brokers Regulatory Association (FIMBRA) to provide advice on arranging and effecting life policies, pension contracts and unit trust investments and is bound by the rules of FIMBRA.
 We offer you independent advice. If, through exceptional circumstances, the Company or any of its directors or registered individuals does have an interest in business you ask us to transact for you, we will write to you with the details of the conflict of interest before we carry out your instructions.
 We normally ask our Clients to give us instructions in writing, to avoid possible disputes. However, we will accept oral instructions provided they are followed up in writing.
 You, or we, may terminate authority to act on your behalf at any time, without penalty. Notice of this termination must be given in writing and will not affect the completion of any transaction already initiated on your behalf.
 ABC Limited receives commission from companies with whom investments (including life assurance) are arranged. We retain that commission and make no charge for our advice or services in arranging life assurance, pension contracts and unit trusts.
 We act as your agents in advising you and arranging investment transactions. We never own the investments which you buy through us. If we receive commission from the issuer of a security or from another intermediary, we will inform you.
 ABC Limited is not authorised to handle Clients' money. This means that we may never accept a cheque made out to the Company. Nor may we handle cash.
 We keep records of all our business transactions for seven years. You (or your agent) may inspect contract notes, vouchers and entries in books (whether kept manually or electronically). We treat all Clients' records as confidential, so we reserve the right to give you copies of your particular records rather than allow access to files containing records about other Clients.
 ABC Limited maintain professional indemnity insurance. This insurance cover has been effected to protect the interests of Clients against professional negligence.
 If at any time you wish to contact me, you can always do so through my head office at the address set out in the heading to this letter. Alternatively, my personal telephone number is shown if you wish to contact me direct.
 As Members of FIMBRA, with effect from the 1st May 1989, we are obliged to advise you that we, as Independent Brokers, will receive commission in respect of business transacted. You will be supplied with information about the commission after completion of the transaction.
 I hope you have found the above helpful and I very much hope that our business relationship will be continued in the future.

Yours sincerely

In signing this document, I confirm I have received a copy of this Terms of Business Letter and a copy of ABC Limited's 'Buyer's Guide'. I confirm I am agreeable to your acting as my Independent Financial Adviser.

Signature..............................
Signature.............................. Partner (if applicable)

Bibliography

Janner, Greville, *Janner on Communication*, Century Business Books.

Janner, Greville, *Janner on Presentation*, Century Business Books.

Kelly, Alan, *Financial Planning for the Individual*, Financial Times Business Information in association with the Institute of Chartered Accountants in England and Wales.

Lewis, David, *The Secret Language of Success (How to read and use body talk)*, Bantam Press (Transworld Publishers Ltd).

Littlefair, Harry (Editor), *Allied Dunbar Investment and Savings Guide*, Longman Group UK Ltd (updated annually).

Reardon, A. M., *Allied Dunbar Pensions Guide*, Longman Group UK Ltd (updated annually).

Reardon, A. M., *Planning your Pension*, Longman Group UK Ltd.

Robinson, Nick, *Persuasive Business Presentations*, Mercury Business Books (distributed by Management Books 2000).

Robson Rhodes, *Personal Financial Planning Manual*, Butterworth and Co (Publishers) Ltd.

Wiles, Tony, *The IFA Marketing Partner*, Management Books 2000.

Young, David, *Working Abroad – The Expatriate's Guide*, Financial Times Business Information.

The Chartered Insurance Institute provides courses in financial planning, aimed at different levels, with study course textbooks which can be bought separately from the courses. They cover:

1. The Financial Planning Certificate
2. The Advanced Financial Planning Certificate.
   Details from: The FPC Unit CII Administrative Office
   31 Hillcrest Road
   London, E18 2JP
   Tel. 081-989 8464
   Fax. 081-530 3052

or: The Chartered Insurance Institute
20 Aldermanbury
London, EC2V 7HY
Tel. 071-606 3835
Fax. 071-726 0131

The Life Insurance Association in partnership with the Chartered Insurance Institute also provides a progressive range of courses and examinations including their Membership by Diploma (equivalent to the FPC) to Associateship and Fellowship. Details from:

Life Insurance Association
862 Citadel House
Chorleywood
Rickmansworth
Herts, WD3 6FP

Useful weekly publications:

Money Marketing
Financial Adviser
Money Week

Useful monthly publications:

Money Management
Pensions Management
Planned Savings
Resident Abroad

Index

Acknowledgment of needs, 62
Advanced financial planning, 11
Advertising and publicity, 187
Advertising Standards Authority, 46, 188
Anecdotes, 145
Appearances and first impression, 14
Apprenticeship, 15
Appropriate solutions, 63
Authorisation by SRO, 180

Background knowledge, 10
Bandler, Richard, 140
Benefits, 63
Best advice, 38, 89, 183, 185
Body language, 169
Buyer's Guide, 60, 183

Chartered Insurance Institute, 11, 205
Client bank, 20
Client excuses, 76
Client meetings, 56
Client profiles, 147
  arrogant clients, 149
  charmers, 151
  pedantic clients, 148
  self-confident clients, 147
  Smart Alecs, 150
  stubborn and illogical clients, 151
Client temperament, 147
Clients' money, 189
Closing the sales, 70
Cold calling, 21, 185
Communication, 153
  answering questions, 166
  brevity, 154
  capturing attention, 159
  clarity of purpose, 155
  communication close, 163
  formulating the right message, 158
  identifying correct listener target, 156
  listening, 168

  non-verbal/body language, 169
  subject matter, 161
  telephone technique, 162
  voice control, 167
Communications skills, 8
Companies Act 1989, 190
Company clients, 33
Competence, 187
Competition, 86
Complaints, 86, 189
Compliance officers, 190
Compliance Rules, 21, 179
Confidence, 6
Confidential questionnaire, 94
Consumer Credit Act 1974, 201
Contacting referred leads, 30
Contents insurance, 93
Continuing Education Programme, 12
Convertible term assurance, 102
Correct procedure, 84
Coué, Emile, 7
Critical illness insurance, 105

Data Protection Act 1984, 199
Deferred decisions, 78
Department of Trade and Industry, 179
Disciplinary action, 190
Discovering your prospect's needs, 62

EC Money Laundering Directive, 201
Economic climate, 174
Economic Secretary to the Treasury, 179
Erikson, Milton, 140
'Execution only', 62
Executive pension plans, 127
Existing clients, 40

Factfinding, 59
Family income benefit, 102
Fear of failure, 7
Feedback, 69
Female prospects, 58

Financial Intermediaries Managers and Brokers Regulatory Association (FIMBRA), 2, 11-13, 123, 180-181, 197, 202-203
Financial Planning Certificate (FPC), 11
Financial products, 1, 97
Financial Services (Clients' Money) Regulations 1987, 189
Financial Services Act, 10, 21, 25, 60, 62, 72, 87-89, 179, 195, 198-199
 amendments, 190
 Section 44(4) and (5), 183
'Fit and proper', 181
Free-standing additional voluntary contribution plans (FSAVC), 116
Friendly Society plan, 68

Goal setting, 17
Goodwill, 40
Greetings, 58
Grinder, John, 140
Group personal pension schemes, 125

Handling objections, 73

Independent financial advisers, 38
Independent intermediaries, 60, 182
Inflation-protected family income benefit, 102
Inflation-protected term assurance, 101
Inheritance tax mitigation, 109
Initial impressions, 57
Insurance Companies Act 1974, 198
Interested parties, 83
Interview techniques, 84
Investments, 91
Investor protection, 21
Irritating traits, 15
Issues of disclosure, 194

Keyman insurance, 108
Know your client, 88, 184
Knowledge of financial planning, 177

LAUTRO-accredited Training and Competence scheme, 11
Legislation, 179

Letters, 34
Level-term assurance, 101
Lewis, Dr David, 57
Liabilities, 93
Life assurance, 61, 97
 peace of mind, 68
Life Assurance and Unit Trust Regulatory Organisation (LAUTRO), 2, 11, 13, 72, 110, 123-124, 180, 186, 194, 197
Life assurance policy, 67
Life Insurance Association, 11, 206
Life policies, 90

Mailshots, 47, 189
Marketing by correspondence, 45
Mental attitude, 6
Metaphors, 145
Misconduct, 190
Misrepresentation Act 1967, 198
Moine, Donald A., 139
Monitoring, 190
Mortgages, 92, 136

Objective pacing, 141
Observation, 15

Pacing, 141
Partnership insurance, 107
Past performance, 46
Pension transfer plans, 119
Pensions, 90, 109
Permanent health insurance, 44, 132
Personal Equity Plans, 68, 92
Personal Investment Authority, 12, 196
Personal pension plans, 111
Polarisation, 180, 182
Preparation, 10
Presentations, 64
Private health insurance, 91
Product belief, 18
Product disclosure, 72, 187
Product features, 63
Product knowledge, 10
Prospect, 20
Prospect decisions, 80
Prospect hesitancy, 85

INDEX

Prospecting, 19
Prospects you know, 26
Psychology of persuasion, 139

Qualified lists, 43

Referred leads, 28
Registered appointed representative, 180
Removal of registration, 190
Reprimands, 190
Right to complain to regulatory bodies, 189
Rules relating to advertising, 45

Sales performance, 174
Savings, 91
Savings and investments plans, 134
School fees, 67
Scripts, 23
Secret Language of Success, The, 57
Secretary of State for Trade and Industry, 179
Section 32 buyout bonds, 121
Securities and Investments Board (SIB), 11, 23, 72, 87, 123, 179-180, 182-183, 185, 190, 192, 194-196
  core rules, 192
Self-employed personal pension plans, 114
Self-regulatory organisations, 179
Selling group schemes, 130
Selling skills, 16
Selling yourself, 58
Skills of persuasion, 139
Social skills, 8
Soft selling, 143
State Earnings-Related Pension Scheme, 90
Statements of principle, 190
Status disclosure, 72
Stories, 145
Strategy/Financial planning, 89
Synchronising with one's audience, 140

Telephone manner, 16
Telephone prospecting, 23
Telephone technique, 28

Termination of authorised firm's membership, 190
Terms of Business letter, 60, 186
TESSA, 92
Tied agents, 38
Time planning, 17
Tips on the profession, 173
Trade Descriptions Act 1968, 198
Training, 10
Treasury, 179
Trusts, 100

Unit-linked whole-of-life policy, 103
Unsolicited calling, 21
Useful words and phrases, 84

Voice, 28

Whole-life with-profit policy, 103
Whole-of-life assurance, 103
Wills, 93
Wives, 39

ALSO AVAILABLE FROM MANAGEMENT BOOKS 2000

The IFA Marketing Partner
Marketing Skills for Client Development
Tony Wiles

(PB, £19.95, 400pp, 290mm x 200mm, ISBN: 1-85252-197-X)

A professional guide for practising IFAs – a complete set of marketing programmes to establish and develop a successful business.

The book contains a number of checklists and exercises to enable IFAs to better identify, quantify and satisfy the needs of clients and prospects. The programmes in *The IFA Marketing Partner* show IFAs how to:-

- identify specific growth markets
- target the right Clients
- discover where to focus effort
- tailor added-value services
- develop cost advantages
- improve Client loyalty
- identify and succeed in new `niches'
- make marketing pay

ABOUT THE AUTHOR
Tony Wiles is a freelance marketing consultant and trainer who specialises in the professional services sector

Recommended by IFA Promotions

'The only comprehensive and immensely practical jargon-free guide to marketing aimed specifically at the IFA' *IFA Promotions*

Available from leading booksellers.
To order by phone, ring 0235-815544 (credit cards accepted)

ALSO AVAILABLE FROM MANAGEMENT BOOKS 2000

Taxation Simplified
89th edition: November Budget 1993
A H Taylor FCCA

(PB, £6.99, 128pp, 190mm x 120mm, ISBN: 0-9508214-7-0)

A concise but thorough explanation of:

- Income Tax
- Corporation Tax
- Capital Allowances
- Capital Gains Tax
- Inheritance Tax
- Value Added Tax

This invaluable potted guide to taxation has been established for many years as a reference tool for laymen and professionals alike. Published annually to reflect the contents of each successive budget, this edition includes the tax changes announced in the most recent (November 1993) budget.

ABOUT THE AUTHOR
A H Taylor is a qualified chartered accountant, who has produced this annual guide for several years.

A recognised and established reference - now in its 89th edition.

Available from leading booksellers.
To order by phone, ring 0235-815544 (credit cards accepted)

ALSO AVAILABLE FROM MANAGEMENT BOOKS 2000

SALES BOOSTER AUDIO CASSETTES

Now the art of salesmanship can be learnt with ease – just sit back and listen as a series of experts explain how to improve your sales performance and get really impressive results.

Whether you are new to sales, embarking on a new aspect of selling or a hardened professional, you will soon discover how easy it is to boost your performance. Each tape is approximately 45 minutes long and includes a special 'Key Points' information card.

1. **How to Make Telephone Appointments Every Time**
2. **How to Make Sure You Close the Sale Every Time**
3. **Selling to Bigger Companies**
4. **How to Sell Effectively on the Telephone / Selling Against Tough Opposition**
5. **Convincing Them with Questions / How to Avoid Negative Thinking**
6. **How to Handle Discount Requests / Cold Calling Made Easier**
7. **How to Improve Business from Telephone Enquiries / How to Maximise Exhibition Sales**
8. **A New Look at Objection Handling**
9. **How to Overcome the Money Objection / The Salesman's Guide to Finance and Accounts**
10. **Negotiation Techniques for the New Salesman / "I could Never be a Salesman"**

Sales Booster Audio Cassettes are the key to sales success. Great value at just £9.99 including VAT.

Available from leading booksellers.
To order by phone, ring 0235-815544 (credit cards accepted)

ALSO AVAILABLE FROM MANAGEMENT BOOKS 2000

Successful Cold Call Selling
2nd Edition
Lee Boyan

(PB, £13.95, 225pp, 228mm x 152mm, ISBN: 0-8144-7718-6)

Over 100 New Ideas, Scripts, and Examples From the US's Foremost Sales Trainer.

Overcome common cold-call fears, find high quality prospects and get them to *want* to see you! Learn how to listen your way to a sale, turn secretaries into allies, sharpen your phone skills, overcome prospects' resistance, smoke screens or procrastination. You'll never have sweaty palms again!

This classic guide shows novices and veterans alike how to conquer the fear of making cold calls, begin a call by first setting and objective, plan the opening move, deal with tough prospects, track down prospects from a variety of sources, get appointments with the right buying authorities, and come across with confidence.

ABOUT THE AUTHOR/PUBLISHER

Lee Boyan is a renowned US sales and marketing consultant, trainer and author, with over 35 years' experience in the field. The book is published by the American Management Association, the world's largest training organisation, and distributed in the UK by Management Books 2000.

"**Ideal for new and veteran sales reps alike, here is the perfect primer for a tough, rewarding job**" *The Wall Street Journal*

Available from leading booksellers.
To order by phone, ring 0235-815544 (credit cards accepted)

ALSO AVAILABLE FROM MANAGEMENT BOOKS 2000

Persuasive Business Presentations
Nick Robinson

(PB, £7.50, 128pp, 216mm x 135mm, ISBN: 1-85252-061-2)

This practical handbook contains a wealth of tested ideas to make your business presentation more powerful - and more profitable.

The book covers all aspects of successful presentation, including:

- preparing the script
- use and interpretation of body language
- stage management
- use of audio-visuals
- coping with disaster

Based on 25 years' experience of selling effectively though personal presentations.

ABOUT THE AUTHOR

As chairman of the Marketing Guild, and founding director of the marketing consultancy Datanews, Nick Robinson has led more than 300 conferences throughout Europe and the US, addressing groups from 100 to as many as 1000. He is also the author of The Marketing Toolkit, a practical guide to alternative marketing techniques (available from Management Books 2000 at £6.99).

"A valuable book for even the best of speakers. Lucid and lively." *Norman Hart, Chairman, International Foundation for Public Relations*

Available from leading booksellers.
To order by phone, ring 0235-815544 (credit cards accepted)

ALSO AVAILABLE FROM MANAGEMENT BOOKS 2000

Close Close Close
John Fenton

(HB, £7.99, 144pp, 234mm x 156mm, ISBN: 1-85252-044-2)

Closing is the most important part of selling and also the hardest. All sales people want to improve their closing techniques – if you can't close, you can't sell.

Written in John Fenton's usual no-nonsense style, this book is crammed full of practical ideas which can be put to use immediately.

With clear and useful lists like the 'Ten Best Closes' and the 'Top Ten Excuses for Not Closing', *Close! Close! Close!* provides an invaluable guide to the techniques which can make the difference between success and failure in the field, including:

- Different ways of closing sales
- How to prepare customers so they are ready to be closed
- How price conditioning affect the close
- Ways of closing sales over the telephone
- How to turn one successful sale into more sales

ABOUT THE AUTHOR
John Fenton is Britain's best-known sales and sales management trainer, dubbed by the media 'The Billy Graham of Selling'.

Available from leading booksellers.
To order by phone, ring 0235-815544 (credit cards accepted)

ALSO AVAILABLE FROM MANAGEMENT BOOKS 2000

The Post-War History of the London Stock Market

George Blakey

(HB, £19.95, 368pp, 246mm x 171mm, ISBN: 1-85251-137-0)

This book charts the course of the London stock market from boom to bust over the last 50 years, including major events such as the Harrods takeover battle, Slater Walker, the Australian nickel boom, Bernie Corfield and the IOS, the Guinness affair, Polly Peck, Robert Maxwell...and all the major economic developments and corporate headlines of the period.

There are now nearly 10 million private investors in the UK plus another 250,000 people professionally involved in the investment business. Very few of them have any knowledge of market history, of past booms and busts, and their causes.

This definitive record of market behaviour set out in readable fashion will become a handbook, a work of reference, comparing bull and bear markets over the past 50 years, their causes and effects. Such a wealth of background information will provide valuable points for discussion when market professionals are talking to clients and, of course, the other way round.

ABOUT THE AUTHOR
George Blakey is a financial journalist and consultant based in London. In the past has worked for a number of banks and investment groups as a financial analyst and is well-known in the City.

Fully endorsed by the Stock Exchange, with a foreword by its chairman

'A valuable reference' *Securities and Investment Review*

'All those with an interest in the investment business will find this book thoroughly enjoyable' *Professional Investor*

Available from leading booksellers.
To order by phone, ring 0235-815544 (credit cards accepted)

ALSO AVAILABLE FROM MANAGEMENT BOOKS 2000

Understanding Finance
Robert Leach

(PB, £9.99, 152pp, 234mm x 153mm, ISBN: 1-85252-028-0)

What does the FT measure, how is it calculated and what does it mean? What is legal tender, and what is the significance of legal tender? How does the tax system work? How do you evaluate pensions? What is the difference between a credit card and a charge card? The various complexities of finance affect us all, yet few of us have a full understanding of:

- Currency and legal tender
- Taxes
- Economic measures
- Interest calculations
- Financial accounting
- Management accounting
- Banking
- Hiring and leasing
- Insurance
- Pensions

ABOUT THE AUTHOR
Robert Leach is a freelance financial writer and a qualified certified accountant with 15 years' experience of working in industry. He is also the author of *Running Your Own Business* (also available from Management Books 2000)

Recommended by the BBC's Moneybox programme

'A complete guide to finance from the basics such as credit and charge cards to sections on pensions, the tax system, accounting and banking' *Banking and Financial Training*

Available from leading booksellers.
To order by phone, ring 0235-815544 (credit cards accepted)